MW00488929

A Time to Protest

*Leadership Lessons from My Father
Who Survived the Segregated South
for 99 Years*

Penny Blue

Life On Purpose Publishing, A Gap Closer Company

SAN ANTONIO, TEXAS

A Time to Protest

*Leadership Lessons from My Father
Who Survived in the Segregated South
for 99 Years*

Copyright © 2020 by **Penny Edwards Blue**
Edited by **Dr. Angela D. Massey**
Cover Design by **pixelstudios**
Back & Interior Photo Credit: **Courtesy of Roanoke Times,
Jared Soares, Photographer (Used by Permission)**
Author Photo by **Charlie Woo Pictures, LLC**

All rights reserved. No part of this publication may be reproduced, distributed or transmitted in any form or by any
means, without prior written permission.

Printed in the United States of America. Except as permitted under the United States Copyright Act of 1976, no part
of this book may be reproduced in any form or by any elec-
tronic or mechanical means including information storage
and retrieval systems—except in the case of brief quotations
in articles or reviews—without the prior written permission
of its publisher, Life on Purpose Publishing and/or Penny E.
Blue

All brand names and product names used in this book are
trademarks, registered trademarks, or trade names of their
respective holders

A Gap Closer ™ Publication
  A Division of Life On Purpose Publishing
  San Antonio, Texas

A Time to Protest/ Penny E. Blue. -- 1st ed.
ISBN 978-1-7336950-5-3

Dedication

I dedicate this book to my parents, who have gone on beyond this physical world, yet have left a warmth, love, strength and legacy that will live through the generations.

Acknowledgments

I would like to thank my parents for the beautiful childhood they provided. I would like to thank my dad for the wonderful stories and my sister Crystal Diane for helping me to capture and document the stories prior to Dad's passing. I would like to thank Linda Carol and Ruby Nadean for the many times they reviewed my manuscript and Ronald Brent for his suggestion of the broken chains on the cover which lead to the overall cover design. In addition, I would like to thank one of my best friends from my "home by the sea," Herbert Evans for his thorough review and suggested direction.

"Those who profess to favor freedom, and yet depreciate agitation, are men who want crops without plowing up the ground."
–FREDERICK DOUGLASS

"One should protest any time there is injustice. The oppressor cannot dictate to the oppressed what to protest or how to protest."

"I have learned from my parents and my ancestors to use what I have and make it work."
–PENNY BLUE

"We stand up for ourselves even if we stand alone."
–MEKIH CINSEAR EDWARDS

Contents

Introduction

I AM A self-proclaimed life-long learner. I believe to be your best you must strive to learn more and love more every day. I strive daily to evolve and reach my goals. My joy comes from helping others to be their best and achieve their goals.

I was born and grew up in the foothills of the Blue Ridge Mountains right outside of Roanoke, Virginia. It is the Moonshine Capital of the World, the land between the lakes—Franklin County, Virginia, specifically Union Hall, Virginia.

I grew up on a farm where we raised tobacco, cows, and pigs. I am number nine of ten children. Ten children in Franklin County was not unusual. There were many families in the area with ten and more children.

My maternal grandmother said I was headed to college from the time I entered the first grade. I am a proud graduate of Hampton University in Hampton, Virginia, "my home by the sea." I obtained an MBA from Duke University, worked for IBM, and retired from IBM as a Delivery Project Executive in 2007 after 25 years of service.

I moved home partially to care for my dad who was 95 at the time. I planned to teach in the local school system—to give back. However, our plans are not always God's plans. After much trial and tribulation over several years, I started my own business *Penny Wise Gateway* in 2015 and currently serve on the local school board.

Often siblings, understandably, ask themselves how in the world their siblings could have grown up in the same household based on how their siblings think and act once they become adults? I am sure my siblings (along with me) have asked that same question many times over the years. Even though children grow up in the same household they have different experiences and sometimes the same experience impacts children differently. In my family since there were ten children spread out over 27 years, it was as if we had three to four different families that definitely grew up in three different decades where America saw a lot of change. As different as we all are, there are two character traits that answer that question for me:

1. We are all hard workers, and we leave no stone unturned; we get the job done.
2. We believe in justice. We don't think that we are better than others, and the only person that has walked this earth better than us is Jesus Christ.

These character traits were embedded in our DNA mainly because our father was a great storyteller and he shared his life experiences with us throughout our childhood and adulthood. He told us great stories of triumph and protest.

Most importantly, he and Mom lived their lives before us in protest.

This book is a book of history—the history of America that helped shape my ancestors and father's environments, along with my father's whose stories of protest helped shape mine and my siblings' lives. It is a collection of the stories that added to our character. It is a collection of stories that pass down his legacy, his father's legacy and his father's fathers' legacy. It is a collection of stories of how an outspoken black man with a fourth-grade education chose to remain in the Jim Crow south during the Great Migration and raise a family that resulted in all ten children graduating high school, eight graduating college, two obtaining MBAs and one obtaining a Doctorate in Education.

In the pages to follow are the stories of an African American male who witnessed people go from traveling on horse and buggy to flying across the country in airplanes. These are the experiences of a man who saw the world go from communicating through letters that traveled through the postal service to faxes, cell phones, and the World Wide Web. These are the protests of a man who was born in a log cabin, rocked in the arms of former slaves, saw the United States go from sharecropping, Jim Crow and lynching to helping elect, gift, and shake the hand of the first African American President.

I helped to create the opportunity for Dad to meet U.S. Presidential candidate, Senator Barack Obama, who went on to become the 44th President of the United States. Dad's meeting President Obama became one of his favorite and latest stories.

..

Preface

Who We Are and Whose We Are

THIS BOOK IS relevant, and a must-read for today for several reasons. You must know who you are and whose you are; when you do, no one else can define you. <u>Healing starts with the truth</u>. Citizens of the United States must have an opportunity to know and understand the authentic history of the United States to have genuine dialogue, healing and true progress toward a more perfect union. Contrary to what America has shown us from the time of our arrival to America's shores in 1619— bound and chained—to us being locked up disproportionately, while police continue to kill us disproportionately amid double unemployment rates, etc., we know that we matter.

The one and only Master created us. When you know you belong to *the* Master of the Universe and know who you are, you refuse to let anyone else define you or subjugate you. You know you were put here for a purpose. This is the legacy Dad and Mom passed on to us by the way they lived their lives and through the stories he passed along. Regardless of what is going on in this country, we matter. "Black Lives Matter." Dad believed that and made sure all his children did as well. He was unafraid to speak up and speak out because he knew that change does not come to the silent.

The Griot's Legacy

While this book focuses on Dad's stories and the historical facts to help you understand why he protested, in no way do I wish to diminish my mother's role in all our lives. As I discovered later in my life, even though Dad appeared to be larger than life, it was Mom and her strength, grace, and beauty that held our family together. This book happens to be about the Griot we had in our midst. As I shared with someone in my life, when I was going through a tough time I needed to talk to my dad. The next question was why not my mom? I responded if I were trying to determine how to set the table, I would talk with Mom. Since I wanted to kick somebody's butt, I needed to talk to Dad.

He lived to be seven weeks shy of 100 years of age. He was born on November 20th, 1912 and passed away October 2, 2012, after a brief stay in a hospital in the Star City of the South, Roanoke, Virginia. You can imagine all that a black man who lived and raised a family in the South for close to 100 years saw and experienced. He didn't just survive; he thrived.

Dad was a prolific storyteller and enjoyed a good story along with a good laugh. He shared many of his life experiences with his ten children through his many stories. As we all grow older and go our separate ways, it is the lessons in the stories that let me know that no matter what happens, these other nine souls are my siblings. The lessons in the stories Dad shared along with how he and Mom lived their lives solidified protest in our souls, in our DNA.

Penny E. Blue
Union Hall, Virginia

CHAPTER 1

Repeating History

ONE OF MY favorite symbols is the Sankofa Bird. Sankofa refers to the Adinkra word from the Akan people of Africa that means we must go back and reclaim our past so that we can move forward. The Sankofa bird looks behind while flying forward so that the past might inform the future journey.

If we look at our history in the United States, we will see that we repeat it on a constant and daily basis. However, most of us are unaware of this repetition, because most of us are not aware of our history. The history taught in our school systems is distorted. It takes much research outside of what is being taught in classrooms to find and understand the true history of the United States.

On the banks of the James River in 1712, Willie Lynch purportedly delivered a speech on how to keep slaves under control for the next 300 years. While the truth of this speech has been questioned—some have even labeled it a hoax—the tactics outlined have been implemented and have worked for more than 300 years. Sadly, they continue to work.

The Willie Lynch Letter

". . . I have a foolproof method for controlling your black slaves. I guarantee every one of you that if installed correctly it will control the slaves for at least 300 years. My method is simple. Any member of your family or your overseer can use it.

Take this simple little list of differences and think about them. On top of my list is "age" but it's there only because it starts with an "A." The second is "COLOR" or shade, there is intelligence, size, sex, size of plantations and status on plantations, attitude of owners, whether the slaves live in the valley, on a hill, East, West, North, South, have fine hair, course hair, or is tall or short. Now that you have a list of differences, I shall give you an outline of action, but before that, I shall assure you that distrust is stronger than trust and envy stronger than adulation, respect or admiration.

The Black slaves after receiving this indoctrination shall carry on and will become self-refueling and self-generating for hundreds of years, maybe thousands. Don't forget you must pitch the old black male vs. the young black male, and the young black male against the old black male. You must use the dark skin slaves vs. the light skin slaves, and the light skin slaves vs. the dark skin slaves. You must use the female vs. the male. And the male vs. the female. You

must also have your white servants and overse-
ers distrust all Blacks. It is necessary that your
slaves trust and depend on us. They must love,
respect and trust only us.

Gentlemen, these kits are your keys to control.
Use them. Have your wives and children use
them, never miss an opportunity. If used in-
tensely for one year, the slaves themselves will
remain perpetually distrustful of each other."

As in the Willie Lynch letter, the strategy of America's wealthy has always been to divide and create discord amongst those of lesser means. The powerful in the United States have always been focused on how to maintain wealth for the few by exploiting all others. They can obtain the cheapest labor possible by sowing discord amongst the races. Whenever it appears blacks are taking a significant leap forward, the power-ful create a "blacklash" by pitting the laborers against each other. While there are many urban definitions of blacklash, I'm using Merriam Webster's definition of backlash with a twist: "a sudden violent backward movement or reaction with the intent of setting black people back."

HISTORICAL BLACKLASHES

The historical references are mentioned to help provide a backdrop for the environment in which Dad and his ancestors lived and worked. One needs to understand how an atmosphere filled with bigotry spurred Dad to protest at every opportunity and share those stories of protest with his children. Also, the backdrop provides the significance of a black man's choice to remain in the segregated South, specifically Virginia, and raise ten children and teach them the importance of speaking up and speaking out against injustice.

The first African slaves were brought to America in 1619. Some Africans were slaves; some were indentured servants. Blacks and whites (slaves and indentured servants) worked and lived side by side for many years.

Slaves were never granted freedom even after working for years. Essentially, once a slave always a slave— slaves had no rights because they were the property of their owner. Indentured servants, on the other hand, could be granted freedom after working an agreed amount of time.

The 1676 Bacon's Rebellion's *blacklash* was slavery for blacks only. Even though slaves and indentured servants worked together, Nathaniel Bacon's Rebellion served as a way for blacks to be classified as slaves and whites to be classified as indentured servants.

Bacon's Rebellion

"Bacon's Rebellion was an armed rebellion in 1676 by Virginia settlers led by Nathaniel Bacon against the rule of Governor William Berkeley. The colony's dismissive policy as it related to the political challenges of its western frontier, along with other challenges including leaving Bacon out of his inner circle, refusing to allow Bacon to be a part of his fur trade with the Indians, and

*Doeg American Indian attacks, helped to moti-
vate a popular uprising against Berkeley, who
had failed to address the demands of the colo-
nists regarding their safety.*

*A thousand Virginians of all classes and races
rose up in arms against Berkeley, attacking Indians, chasing Berkeley from Jamestown,
Virginia, and ultimately torching the capital.
The rebellion was first suppressed by a few
armed merchant ships from London whose cap-
tains sided with Berkeley and the loyalists.
Government forces from England arrived soon
after and spent several years defeating pockets
of resistance and reforming the colonial government to be once more under direct royal
control."*

The response to the rebellion was to create
laws to divide and conquer to ensure this type of
uprising did not reoccur. Whites became indentured servants; Africans became slaves, and
Indians were put on reservations. By 1700, 15% of
Virginia's population was enslaved Africans.

Given the number of slaves, the slave labor outpaced the indentured servant labor and was much more profitable.

THE CIVIL WAR'S "BLACKLASH" WAS THE KKK AND SHARECROPPING

Before the ink was dry on Commander Robert E. Lee's surrender to General Ulysses S. Grant in Appomattox, Virginia, the treasonous formed the Ku Klux Klan in Tennessee. Southern whites were unwilling to give up their slaves, so they found another way to keep them without calling it slavery: it was called terrorism.

Experts tell us that "terrorism erodes the sense of security and safety people usually feel. This erosion of security is at both the individual level and the community level. Terrorism challenges the natural need of human beings to see the world as predictable, orderly, and controllable. Research has shown that deliberate violence creates longer lasting mental health effects than natural disasters or accidents." Once the KKK was created, Blacks had no security. Individuals and families lived under constant threat from America's home-grown terrorists—a home-grown terrorist that the U.S. government has refused to diffuse.

The Roots of the Ku Klux Klan

"The Ku Klux Klan commonly called the KKK or simply the Klan, refers to three distinct secret movements at different points in time in the history of the United States. Each has advocated extremist reactionary positions such as white supremacy, white nationalism, anti-immigration.

Historically, the KKK used terrorism—both physical assault and murder—against groups or individuals whom they opposed. All three movements have called for the "purification" of American society and all are considered right-wing extremist organizations. In each era, membership was secret and estimates of the total were highly exaggerated by both the friends and enemies.

The first Klan flourished in the Southern United States in the late 1860s, then died out by the early 1870s. It sought to overthrow the Republican state governments in the South during the Reconstruction Era, especially by using violence against African American leaders."

The second group was founded in the South in 1915 and it flourished nationwide in the early and mid-1920s, including urban areas of the Midwest and West. Taking inspiration from D. W. Griffith's 1915 silent film The Birth of a Nation, which mythologized the founding of the first Klan, it employed marketing techniques and a popular fraternal organization structure. Rooted in local Protestant communities, it sought to maintain white supremacy, often took a pro-prohibition stance, and it opposed Catholics and Jews, while also stressing its opposition to the Catholic Church at a time of high immigration from the mostly Catholic nations of Central Europe and Southern Europe.

This second organization was funded by selling its members a standard white costume. It used K-words which were similar to those used by the first Klan, while adding cross burnings and mass parades to intimidate others. It rapidly declined in the latter half of the 1920s.

The third and current manifestation of the KKK emerged after 1950, in the form of localized and isolated groups that use the KKK name. They have focused on opposition to the civil rights movement, often using violence and murder to suppress activists. It is classified as a hate group by the Anti-Defamation League and the Southern Poverty Law Center. As of 2016, the Anti-Defamation League puts total Klan membership nationwide at around 3,000, while the Southern Poverty Law Center (SPLC) puts it at 6,000 members total.

Many plantations went from slavery to sharecropping. Plantation owners entered into contractual agreements with their previous slaves. Many of the once enslaved never left the plantation of their master. Yes, they were set free on paper without the benefit of any compensation for their previous 250 years of work. Most had only known the hard work of the fields and remained on the plantation under a losing contract. A contract which kept them poor, barely fed and in debt to the farm owner. A system not much better than the system of slavery that had just been overthrown by the shedding of blood. And of course, there was the KKK to keep everybody in their places. Since the sharecroppers were on the losing end of the contract, they were never able to get ahead and had to remain on the farm to pay a debt that could never be paid off.

RECONSTRUCTION'S "BLACKLASH" WAS JIM CROW

African Americans began to make tremendous progress after the signing of the 14th Amendment and during the Reconstruction period. Research reveals that, "After the Civil War, with the protection of the Thirteenth, Fourteenth, and Fifteenth Amendments to the Constitution and the Civil Rights Act of 1866, African Americans enjoyed a period when they could vote, actively participate in the political process, acquire the land of former owners, seek employment of their own, and use public accommodations. Opponents of this progress, however, soon rallied against the former slaves' freedom and began to find means for eroding the gains for which many had shed their blood."

In the state of Virginia, The General Assembly refused to ratify the 14th Amendment. The only way Virginia could regain representation in Congress was to ratify the Amendment on October 8, 1869, more than a year after it had become part of the Constitution. In the meantime, whites were busy creating ways to intimidate and overpower people of color.

The History of Jim Crow

"Jim Crow laws were state and local laws that enforced racial segregation in the Southern United States. Enacted by white Democratic-dominated state legislatures in the late 19th cen-

tury after the Reconstruction period, these laws continued to be enforced until 1965. They mandated racial segregation in all public facilities in the states of the former Confederate States of America, starting in the 1870s and 1880s, and upheld by the United States Supreme Court's "separate but equal" doctrine for African Americans. Public education had essentially been segregated since its establishment in most of the South after the Civil War.

This principle was extended to public facilities and transportation, including segregated cars on interstate trains and, later, buses. Facilities for African Americans were consistently inferior and underfunded compared to those which were then available to white Americans; sometimes they did not exist at all.

This body of law institutionalized a number of economic, educational, and social disadvantages. Segregation by law existed mainly in the Southern states, while Northern segregation was generally a matter of fact—patterns of

housing segregation enforced by private cove-
nants, bank lending practices, and job
discrimination, including discriminatory labor
union practices. "Jim Crow" was a pejorative
expression referring to a minstrel song called
"Jump Jim Crow" by a performer appearing in
blackface."

The Jim Crow "blacklash" was spawned by the 1877 Compromise which ended Reconstruction and instituted the southern Jim Crow laws which were enforced by the government and the KKK.

In the North, there were no Jim Crow laws, just Jim Crow practices which created African American housing projects. Thus, African Americans suffered through 100 years of Jim Crow slavery.

MODERN DAY CIVIL RIGHTS "BLACKLASH" IS THE CORPORATE PRISON SYSTEM

The 1964 Civil Rights Act struck down the most visible signs of Jim Crow. The "blacklash" moved to use the tactics the North, West and other parts of the country had already been utilizing. They were and still are tactics more challenging to identify and prove, such as redlining, private schools, school vouchers, police brutality, racist employment, driving while black, profiling, drug and gun laws, lax integration laws and enforcement because of the need to replace cheap labor.

David A. Love and Vijay Das explain how the prison system continues to contribute to "blacklash," and how greedy corporations profit from this corrupt system.

Slavery and the U.S. Prison System

"Slavery persists by another name today. Young men and women of colour toil away in 21st-century fields, sow in hand. And Corporate America is cracking the whip.

Influenced by enormous corporate lobbying, the United States Congress enacted the Prison Industry Enhancement Certification Program in 1979 which permitted US companies to use prison labour. Coupled with the drastic increase in the prison population during this period, profits for participating companies and revenue for the government and its private contractors soared. The Federal Bureau of Prisons now runs a programme called Federal Prison Industries (UNICOR) that pays inmates under one dollar an hour. The programme generated $500m in sales in 2016 with little of that cash being passed down to prison workers. Stateside, where much of the US addiction to mass incarceration lies, is no different. California's prison labour programme is expected to produce some $232m in sales in 2017.

These exploited labourers are disproportionately African American and Latino—a demographic status quo resulting from the draconian sentencing and other criminal justice policies ransacking minority communities across the

United States. <u>African Americans are incarcerated at a rate five times higher than that</u> of <u>whites</u>. In states like Virginia and Oklahoma, one in every 14 or 15 African American men are put in prison.

We lock people of colour up at alarming rates. We put them to work. Corporations gain. This story is an age-old American tradition."

THE PRESIDENT OBAMA "BLACKLASH" IS THE CURRENT POLITICAL CLIMATE AND TRUMP

Any student of history should not have been surprised by the election of Donald Trump. Furthermore, no one should be surprised by Donald Trump's disrespect of President Obama and his political legacy. *NYMag* writer, Jonathan Chait put it this way, "There has never been an American president so consumed with envy at his predecessor as Donald Trump. Consequently, there has never been a president whose legacy has been scrutinized in quite the same way as Barack Obama."

The historical blacklashes have had far-reaching effects on African Americans economic growth. The 2016 U.S. Census Bureau data identified African Americans as "the only racial group that has been left behind."

The Discriminatory Wage Gap

"Williams Rodgers, chief economist at the Heldrich Center for Workforce Development at Rutgers University... co-wrote a report... that found that black-white wage gaps are larger today than they were in 1979.

The study noted that even when African Americans attend college and actively work to expand their skills and networks, they still earn far less than whites with a similar educational background. In fact, the wage gap has expanded the most between college-educated blacks and whites.

His conclusion after years of looking at the data and trends: "Wage gaps are growing primarily because of discrimination," Rodgers said."

Despite the blacklashes previously noted and in some cases, because of the blacklashes, my father taught us that the wise pay attention to their history and make the necessary changes to ensure a brighter future. Remember, when you know your history, it allows you to see current events more clearly and respond in a more definitive and appropriate manner.

CHAPTER 2

Roots: The Family Tree

FREEDOM HAS BEEN hard fought for and must continue to be fought for on an on-going basis. I have never read in history where the King or the powerful woke up one morning and said, "I'm tired of being King" or "I'm tired of being so powerful, I think I'll allow someone else to take my place."

As human beings, we have the three big Ts to give: Time, Talent and Treasure. If you are not investing your time, talent and treasure for freedom, you are allowing yourself and your children to spend that time, talent, and treasures en-slaved. Dad believed this, lived by this and passed it on to his ten children. He knew there was a time to protest. He protested loud and long until change finally came.

THE FAMILY TREE

My dad's paternal grandparents were Abron Edwards and Fannie Dickerson. Abron is the language of the Abron people and a major dialect of the Akan language of Central Ghana. Many people speak it in Central Ghana.

Abron and Fannie's names show up for the first time in the 1870 census which is typical for many slaves/African Americans in the South. Their ages were 21 and 18 respectively. They were both living in a home with many other people. There is no documentation about the relationship of all the people living in the one house. However, since it was only five years after the Civil War, it can be surmised that many blacks lived together to survive and make a living.

Dad's maternal grandparents were Charles Mattox and Lucy Ann Dunnings, and both were considered colored on their marriage license; ages 24 and 18 respectfully. They were married December 1st, 1870. Lucy and her family were part of the free blacks living in Franklin County, Virginia. Charles was of mixed lineage. He is listed on the 1870 census as a mulatto. His father was a white farmer, Samuel Mattox. His mother was a black woman, Sallie Ann listed as a housekeeper who lived next door to Sam.

Before the end of the Civil War, Sallie Ann was Sam Mattox's slave and appears to have been 22 years younger than Sam. A common practice during this time was Master-Slave relations.

Master-Slave Relations

"Slave women were forced to comply with sexual advances by their masters on a very regular basis. Consequences of resistance often came in the form of physical beatings; thus, an enormous number of slaves became concubines for these

men. Most often the masters were already bound in matrimony, which caused tension and hatred between the slave and the mistress of the house. Many "mulatto" or racially mixed children also resulted from these relations. Because the "status of the child" followed that of his or her mother, the child of a white man would not be freed based upon patriarchal genealogy. These children also became a sore reminder for the mistress of her husband's infidelity.

The following passages sketch the nature of the master-slave relations, and their consequences:

"Maria was a thirteen-year-old house servant. One day, receiving no response to her call, the mistress began searching the house for her. Finally, she opened the parlor door, and there was the child with her master. The master ran out of the room, mounted his horse and rode off to escape, 'though well he knew that [his wife's] full fury would fall upon the young head of his victim.'

The mistress beat the child and locked her up in a smokehouse. For two weeks the girl was constantly whipped. Some of the elderly servants attempted to plead with the mistress on Maria's behalf, and even hinted that 'it was mass'r that was to blame.' The mistress's reply was typical: 'She'll know better in the future. After I've done with her, she'll never do the like again, through ignorance.'" (Stanley Felstein, Once a Slave: The Slaves' View of Slavery, p.132).

Here, the mistress was able to take out her aggressions on the girl rather than the guilty master. I suppose we could empathize with the frustration and betrayal these wives felt, but the outlet of their aggressions often became the slave girl. Women in the south were quite powerless. Because the option of divorce was not readily available, the mistresses often times punished the slave women for their husbands' wrongdoings."

According to my research, Sam and Sallie Ann had four children. Sallie Ann had two children with her husband, John Willis Muse. And of course, the master, Sam, had children by his wife. Many of their descendants (both black and white) live in Union Hall and Franklin County today and have for generations.

As you can see based on my dad's grandparents, these were extraordinary times. However, this is the history of most blacks in the South, and it is the history of most blacks in America.

The oldest story Dad shared with us was about his Grandpa Charles. As noted, Grandpa Charles' father was also his and his mother's master, Sam Mattox. Not to break with custom and tradition during those times, the master had two families. He had his white family by his wife who lived in his home and his black family, by his slave(s); therefore, the children from this union were slaves.

The Good Boy

Sam Mattox use to sit back and say "Ples is a good boy. Dent is a good boy. Well, Charles is a good boy, too."

Ples and Dent were Sam's sons by his wife. Based on this, there must have been some acknowledgment of the two families.

Dad was very close to his grandparents and lived near his maternal grandparents. The property they lived on and owned is back in our family today. Two of my siblings and I purchased the land in 2009.

A second story my dad shared was about the land and his Grandpa Charles and Charles' dad/master.

The Land Inheritance Story

Sam Mattox shared with Charles that he was leaving him some land. However, when he showed Charles the land he was leaving each of his sons, Ples and Dent's land was nice and flat. The land he was leaving to Charles was in a holler. Once seeing the land, Charles told his dad not to bother. Charles told him to keep his land and he would work and buy his own damn land!

My father's grandparents, which he knew intimately, were legally granted their freedom and citizenship by the Civil War and the 13th and 14th amendments.

Forty Acres and a Mule

"Forty acres and a mule refer to a promise made in the United States for agrarian reform for former enslaved black farmers by Union General William Tecumseh Sherman on January 16, 1865. It followed a series of conversations between Secretary of War Edwin M. Stanton and Radical Republican abolitionists Charles Sumner and Thaddeus Stevens following disruptions to the institution of slavery provoked by the American Civil War. Many freedmen believed and were told by various political figures that they had a right to own the land they had long worked as slaves, and were eager to control their own property. Freed people widely expected to legally claim 40 acres (16 ha) of land (a quarter-quarter section) and a mule after the end of the war, long after proclamations such as

Sherman's Special Field Orders, No. 15 and the Freedmen's Bureau Act were explicitly reversed.

Some land redistribution occurred under military jurisdiction during the war and for a brief period thereafter. However, federal and state policy during the Reconstruction era emphasized wage labor, not land ownership, for blacks. Almost all land allocated during the war was restored to its pre-war owners. Several black communities did maintain control of their land, and some families obtained new land by homesteading. Black land ownership increased markedly in Mississippi during the 19th century, particularly. The state had much undeveloped bottomland behind riverfront areas that had been cultivated before the war. Most blacks acquired land through private transactions, with ownership peaking at 15,000,000 acres (6,100,000 ha) in 1910, before an extended financial recession caused problems that resulted in the loss of their property for many."

The slaves were promised 40 acres and a mule. They received neither. As a people, they had been enslaved for 246 years . . . for 246 years, they had been denied an education, denied compensation for their labor, and treated like animals.

As history confirms, the U.S. promised the newly freedman many things that never came to fruition. They were set free with no benefits from their 246 years of labor and no support or direction on how to move forward. Instead, they faced questionable tactics put in place to ensure that they could *not* move forward; this was the landscape in Virginia for Dad's grandparents. Still, they chose to thrive and survive without the promised 40 acres and a mule. They chose to endure hardships to ensure that their children were free in mind, body, and spirit.

Silent Protest

I Can Buy My Own!

My paternal grandfather, Edmond King Edwards, lived on a white man's farm where he worked. When he was 18, the white man told him that if he stayed on with them and worked hard when he turned 21, they would give him a horse and a saddle. My grandfather told the farmer, "If I work hard for myself when I turn 21, I will buy my own horse and saddles!"

My grandfather was born 1886, 21 years after the Civil War and nine years after Reconstruction.

On July 8, 1903, Grandpa Edmond King and his two brothers, W. Henry and Wiley J. purchased 100 acres of land from a Byrd family from Roanoke, Virginia. The entire contract is listed in a handwritten deed in the Franklin County Court House. The purchase amount was $450.00. They made a cash payment of $50.00 and then additional payments over a two-year period. Later,

Grandpa purchased his brothers' interest. This property is still in our family today.

Grandpa's vision for himself and his family allowed him to own a beautiful 100-acre farm full of orchards, apples, grapevines, and animals, including horses and chickens. First, he built a log cabin on the land; later he built a beautiful two-story home.

The farm was a beautiful setting. One could reach the house from a long road descending to flat valley area (the bottom). As you approached the house, you passed by an immaculately kept tobacco barn at the top of the hill on the right. Then you approached a large stable for horses on the left that connected to my Aunt Betty's land. The next building is what folk called a pack house where tools and odds and ends were kept. There was a parking space and a cement walk that took you to a beautiful white two-story home with a large cement porch and columns. On the porch was a swing that hung from the ceiling, along with some other free-standing porch furniture.

A weeping willow tree and grapevines graced the yard. There was a large chicken coop below the grapevines. On the opposite side of the house was a hog pen. Behind this lovely home was an orchard and further below the orchard was what we called "the bottom." A creek ran through it and the land in the bottom was more fertile than the land closer to the house. Grandpa used this land to grow acres and acres of Virginia's cash crop, tobacco. There was also an outhouse. However, the home had an inside toilet.

When you entered the home, there was a foyer with a staircase leading to two large bedrooms upstairs. Downstairs to the right was a large living room. My grandparent's bedroom was to the left and a hall that led to the bathroom and the back of the house. In the back of the house were an enclosed porch, large kitchen and a dining room that connected the kitchen and living room. We mostly approached my grandparents' house over the hills and through the woods.

My grandfather and other black men took great pride in their land. It allowed them to show others they were men also. Further, it gave them the opportunity that had previously been denied them—something of their own. It felt good to be the boss and work for themselves. Farming is one of the earliest forms of entrepreneurship.

Grandpa and other men in the area worked their farms in the summer and traveled to West Virginia in the winter to work in the coal mines where they were able to work and make enough money to seed their entrepreneurship hopes and dreams. They poured their blood, sweat, and tears into their land. It was land ownership that helped identify them as equal to white men. It was something that engulfed all their senses; something they could feel and smell. It was their road to equality. Owning land gave them additional rights only granted to landowners. It helped place them one step closer to justice in an unjust world.

Sometimes we can protest an injustice designed to keep us down by rising and taking control of our lives. Grandpa did just that and led by example when he refused to work for a horse and saddle. Through his actions, he showed his children that hard work, vision, and a refusal to bow is often the loudest protest. He passed the spirit of protest on to my father.

Freedom is Not Free

IN 1860, ONE year before the beginning of the Civil War, it is estimated the value of all slaves in the South was $3B. The U.S. Gross National Product was only $4B. Therefore, the Civil War was undoubtedly about how to divide and increase the $3B pie through the expansion of slavery.

History shows the North and South both benefited greatly from the slave trade. Slavery became an issue as America expanded west. Each new territory was defined as a slave territory or non-slave territory and many times led to physical battle. Well known congressional settlements for this matter are *The Missouri Compromise* and the *Kansas-Nebraska Act.*

Many argue soldiers like Robert E. Lee, etc., said they were fighting for Virginia and/or their respective state. All soldiers fight for their country, their flag. However, it is the elected officials of the government that determine the purpose of the war, not the soldiers. Others argue the Civil War was about commerce and/or states' rights. It was about both. Slavery was the commerce and the states' rights were the states' rights to own slaves. This is documented in the southern states' succession speeches.

During the Civil War, President Lincoln approached this topic very carefully, because the North was not interested in giving their lives on the battlefield to free the Africans, nor did they want the Africans to live among them. President Lincoln put pen to paper that he intended to win the war and preserve the Union whether that freed the Africans from slavery or whether they remained in bondage.

In his August 22, 1862 letter written to Horace Greely, Lincoln made that point clear.

The Horace Greely Letter

"My paramount object in this struggle is to save the Union, and is not either to save or to destroy slavery. If I could save the Union without freeing any slave I would do it, and if I could save it by freeing all the slaves I would do it; and if I could save it by freeing some and leaving others alone, I would also do that. What I do about slavery, and the colored race, I do because I believe it helps to save the Union; and what I forbear, I forbear because I do not believe it would help to save the Union. I shall do less whenever I shall believe what I am doing hurts the cause and I shall do more whenever I shall believe doing more will help the cause."

However, black folks were determined to participate in the war and to be free at the end of the war. Because of the population imbalance between the Northern and Southern states, along with the South's dependency on the North, President Lincoln and the North thought this to be a short, decisive battle.

The South utilized their slaves to fuel their war machine. According to the U.S. 1860 census, the total country population was 31,443,321. The North was comprised of 22,443,321 while the South had only 9,000,000. Included in the population numbers were 430,000 slaves in the North and 3,530,000 slaves in the South. The numbers also included free blacks.

In the beginning, neither the North, nor South allowed blacks to participate as soldiers. The South utilized their slaves on the home front as food producers and factory foremen which allowed the South to send a larger percentage of white men to the war effort. They also utilized their slaves in the actual war effort as teamsters, cooks, body servants, and medics. Slaves built the fortifications, dug the ditches, prepared the battlefield, etc.

TACTICS TO WIN A WAR

THE CONFISCATION ACTS

It was Fredrick Douglas that continued to press Lincoln to allow African American soldiers to participate in the war effort. President Lincoln and Congress did everything possible to win the war until they had no choice but to agree with Douglass. Once African Americans entered the war as soldiers, President Lincoln and General Grant both determined it was the fighting power of African American men that turned the war to the North's favor.

Lincoln's August 26, 1863 Conkling Letter

"The war has certainly progressed as favorably for us, since the issue of proclamation as before. I know, as fully as one can know the opinions of others, that some of the commanders of our

armies in the field who have given us our most important successes believe the emancipation policy and the use of the colored troops constitute the heaviest blow yet dealt to the Rebellion, and that at least one of these important successes could not have been achieved when it was but for the aid of black soldiers."

Many northern and southern generals and soldiers stated they were fighting for their state. African American soldiers were fighting for their life. They were fighting for their freedom. They were fighting for their dignity. They were fighting for the life, freedom, and dignity of their children and their children to come. President Lincoln and Congress tried a number of war maneuvers before allowing African Americans to participate in the Union Army as soldiers.

For example, in 1861, Congress passed *The Confiscation Act* to permit courts to seize *any* property being used to support the Confederate's determination to expand slavery, including slaves. This act gave the Union generals the right to keep captured slaves as contraband during the battle versus returning them to the Confederate Army to allow them to continue to be used as workhorses and power the Confederate Army.

On July 17, 1862, Congress passed the second Confiscation Act which further strengthened Act I and set the foundation for the Emancipation Proclamation. It stated that slaves of civilian and military Confederate officials "shall be forever free," but it was enforceable only in areas of the South occupied by the Union Army. President Lincoln was again concerned about the effect of an antislavery measure on the border states and again urged these states to begin gradual compensated emancipation.

According to the *NY Times*, President Lincoln also signed a Militia Act on the same day which allowed the Union Army to enlist and utilize blacks in the Union Army. The Act helped the Union military because freed slaves served as spies and supplied the Union Army with information that helped them gain strategic advantages. Any time the Union Army got within close proximity of slaves, many fled the plantation and followed the Army.

At Fort Huachuca Army Base Intelligence Museum in Sierra Vista, Arizona there is a statue of Harriet Tubman representing the intelligence she and other African Americans provided the Union Army in the war efforts. She served as a nurse and spy. Many others served as spies and provided the Union Army the intelligence to help them win the war effort. Another unsung hero was John Scobell, a highly trained operative who quietly gathered information for the Union Army. It's been said that the Confederate's disregard for their slaves was a tactical weakness.

THE EMANCIPATION PROCLAMATION

The Emancipation Proclamation was another ingenious war maneuver/tactic by President Lincoln. It came after the first and second Confiscation Acts and only after Frederick Douglas' unremitting push for the President to allow blacks to participate in the Civil War as soldiers.

The Ebony Pictorial History of Black America
on The Emancipation Proclamation

"The Emancipation Proclamation was a decisive factor in the Civil War. A child of military necessity and political pressure, the Proclamation changed the tone of the war and gave the North the added power it needed to crush the Southern war effort."

On December 31, 1862, blacks all over the country gathered in churches and homes awaiting the anticipated Emancipation Proclamation. This anticipation was the beginning of "Watch Night" services practiced in African American churches all over the country to this day. Once the Emancipation Proclamation arrived, there were prayers, shouts, and songs of joy as people fell to their knees and thanked God. We still gather in churches all over the country and thank God for helping us through the past year and pray for His continued coverage into the new year.

Enacted on January 1, 1863, The Emancipation Proclamation freed the 3,530,000 slaves in the Confederate territory but did not free the 430,000 slaves in the Union territory.

The Civil War came to an end in Appomattox, Virginia which is 71 miles from Union Hall, Virginia (Franklin County) where my great grandparents were enslaved. The battle that ended in Appomattox, Virginia began from General Grant's headquarters in City Point in Petersburg, Virginia and was led by African American men that came through and torched or burned down Richmond, Virginia (the capital of the Confederacy) and continued west to Appomattox, Virginia where General Robert E. Lee surrendered to General Ulysses S. Grant.

What was on the slave grapevine in Franklin County? Were my grandparents aware the battle was headed west toward Franklin County? Were they aware that Richmond had been captured and burned to the ground? Was there discussion of should they run and follow the Union Army as hundreds of other slaves did when the Union Army came near? How long did it take for the news to get to Union Hall that General Lee surrendered to General Grant just 70 miles away? What was their reaction?

If anybody in America should be celebrating and erecting statues for the heroic efforts and conclusion of the Civil War, it should be black folk celebrating their freedom after 246 years of chattel slavery, their ongoing pursuit of freedom, not settling for no, their demand to participate in the battle for their freedom, along with their gallant service in the battle.

CHAPTER 4

Short-Lived Changes

DURING THE SAME year the Civil War ended and before President Lincoln's assassination, the 13th amendment of the United States Constitution was passed.

It was President Lincoln's ingenuity again that helped push the Amendment through Congress which officially freed African Americans from slavery.

The 14th Amendment, a Reconstruction Amendment, of the United States Constitution was ratified in 1868 which granted black men full citizenship and equal protection under the law, but the Amendment did not pass through Congress with ease. It was a hard-fought battle and still wages today.

The leverage in 1868 was that the Confederate States had to ratify the Amendment to regain representation in Congress. However, it was debated fiercely among the Northern states as well. New Jersey, Ohio, and Oregon voted to ratify and later decided to rescind their votes. The federal government had to send troops to enforce the 13th and 14th Amendments in the South.

During the Reconstruction years (1865 to 1877) blacks voted, won elected office and served on juries throughout the nation, including the South. It appeared that things had changed.

The Appearance of Change

"After the Civil War, the Reconstruction Era (1865-1877) brought enormous change to America's political life.

"Reconstructed" southern state governments, new laws, and constitutional amendments all expanded voting rights for African American men. But by the 1880s as federal intervention diminished, most southern states prevented African American men from voting by using a combination of laws, economic pressure, and intimidation; most African Americans in the South only regained real access to the polls in the 1960s.

For example, in Minnesota, Black men won the right to vote in 1868 during Reconstruction. Many slaves had escaped the South via the Mississippi River to Minnesota earlier in the 1800s. But it wasn't until after the Civil War—in which Black Minnesotans had served—that African American men achieved suffrage.

In the Civil War years (1861-1865) the focus was on winning the war. During those years abolition of slavery was a very contentious issue, and Black suffrage took a back seat. But after the war, voting rights advocates sought a change in the Minnesota constitution to guarantee Black suffrage. The procedure for amending the constitution had two steps: the legislature had to vote to submit an amendment to the people, and the people had to vote to pass the amendment. The Golden Key Club, a St. Paul literary group for Black men, was one organization that lobbied the state legislature for Black voting rights.

In 1865, 1867 and 1868 the legislature voted to submit a referendum on Black suffrage to the voters. Then-Governor William Marshall, a Republican, supported the 1867 and 1868 referendums. The first two times, in 1865 and 1867, the suffrage referendum was defeated. In 1865 the referendum lost by 2,513 votes out of 26,789 cast. But in 1867 it lost by a far smaller margin, 1,298 votes out of 56, 220 votes cast. One reason for the 1867 defeat might have been that the referendum question was written on a separate ballot that several thousand voters apparently overlooked.

In other parts of the country, Black voting rights made big gains in 1867. Black residents of the District of Columbia and of all federal territories gained the right to vote. Also, Congress required that, as a condition to being readmitted to the Union, all former Confederate states had to guarantee Black males the right to vote. Nebraska was also required to guarantee Black men voting rights in order to be admitted as a new state."

Although, General Lee surrendered to General Grant at Appomattox Court House in Appomattox, Virginia, the United States has yet to surrender white supremacy and has yet to grant black men full citizenship and equal protection under the law.

RECONSTRUCTION AND JIM CROW (1865 – 1876)

The unprecedented presidential election of 1876 provided the South the opportunity to put blacks back in their place and reinstitute the next form of slavery: Jim Crow, enforced by the Ku Klux Klan.

Whenever, it appears that blacks are making a significant amount of progress, whites forge severe "blacklash."

White Supremacy

"White elites, cast out of power and facing policies that threatened their economic hold on the state, launched a campaign that they knew would drive blacks and whites apart. They called it a campaign of "white supremacy," and sought to unite whites of all economic backgrounds in hatred of black people. It was this campaign that tried to re-enforce the idea of black people as different, as lesser, and as a race that had to be separate from whites. Segregation was created in the South during this time period, and many of the ideas that drove it still exist more than a century later . . . "

Politicians campaign and often win elections based on fear. The 1870s was racked with depression making it easy to appeal to white voters fearful of losing their jobs.

The Compromise of 1877 resulted in the Federal Government withdrawing troops from the South which put an end to Reconstruction; thus, terrorism became the law of the land. The Compromise of 1877 was a deal struck by the Democratic and Republican parties on the backs of black men to settle a bitter legal and political battle resulting from the 1877 presidential campaign.

The Democratic candidate outpolled the Republican candidate and had the majority of undisputed electoral votes. The disputed electoral votes were awarded to Rutherford B. Hayes, the Republican candidate, who became the 19th president of the United States. The Federal Government removed the Federal Troops from the South that had been placed there after the Civil War to protect law and order—to protect blacks.

Terror once again was the law of the land for the South. The more things changed, the more they stayed the same. In the case of blacks, things became worse. Over the next 20 plus years Jim Crow laws were established and confederate statues erected state by state all over the South to halt black progress and further establish white supremacy to keep blacks in slavery.

JIM CROW LAWS BY STATE

South Carolina: Black and White textile workers could not work in the same room, or enter through the same door, gaze out of the same window. Many industries would not hire blacks and labor unions passed rules to exclude blacks.

Virginia: In Richmond, one could not live on a street unless most of the residents were people one could marry. Until 1967 it was against the law to marry someone of a different race.

Interracial Marriage in Virginia

Loving v. Virginia, 388 U.S. 1 (1967) is a land-mark civil rights decision of the United States Supreme Court, which invalidated laws prohibiting interracial marriage.

The case was brought by Mildred Loving (née Jeter), a woman of color, and Richard Loving, a white man, who had been sentenced to a year in prison in Virginia for marrying each other. Their marriage violated the state's anti-miscegenation statute, the Racial Integrity Act of 1924, which prohibited marriage between people classified as "white" and people classified as "colored," The Supreme Court's unanimous decision determined that this prohibition was unconstitutional, overruling Pace v. Alabama (1883) and ending all race-based legal restrictions on marriage in the United States.

Virginia told fraternal social groups that black and white members could not address each other as "Brother."

Texas: Entire towns prohibited blacks from living in the town.

Alabama: Mobile prohibited blacks from leaving their homes after 10 p.m.

Georgia: Had separate parks for blacks and whites, Atlanta courts kept two Bibles: one for black witnesses and one for whites

Oklahoma: Had separate phone booths for blacks and whites.

Throughout the South signs marked "Whites Only" or "Colored" hung over doors, ticket windows, and drinking fountains. Schools, colleges, prisons, hospitals, and orphanages were segregated. "Signs were used to show non-whites where they could legally walk, talk, drink, rest, or eat. Segregated facilities extended from white only schools to white only graveyards."

Dad had a few stories that he passed on to us that illustrate the effects of Jim Crow. However,

he nor my Uncle Lester were men to bow to in-
justices heaped on them because of Jim Crow.

West Virginia Dining Room: We Serve Blacks, But...

Throughout the South most restaurants and public places practiced Jim Crow. Blacks were not served in the dining area of the restaurant. They could purchase food to go or sometimes there was a separate dining area for them to eat.

Dad did not patronize establishments that did not serve blacks in the dining area or where they did not feel welcomed. Most of the time when blacks traveled they either packed food to eat or did without.

Occasionally, there were establishments that served blacks.

Dad and others made many trips to and from West Virginia on a regular basis. Their work was in West Virginia and their families were in Virginia. Based on today's travel it is about a three-hour drive. During this timeframe it was much longer—about a six-hour drive.

On one occasion, Dad and several men were on their way to West Virginia and were caught out on the road without a packed meal. Naturally, they were hungry and wanted some breakfast, so they decided to stop at a restaurant on the chance that the restaurant served blacks. When they entered the restaurant, Dad ask the lady if they served Blacks. She replied yes and proceeded to take their order. Once the orders were ready, she came out and told Dad and the other men that their orders were ready, and they could come on back in the kitchen and eat. The conversation went like this:

"You said you served blacks."

"We do, but not in the dining room. We serve them in the kitchen."

"Lady, I don't eat in my own damn kitchen!"

He then walked out, and the other men followed.

Before Rosa Parks there was Uncle Lester

Uncle Lester was on his way from Ivan Hoe, Virginia to Bluefield, West Virginia on the bus. He got on the bus, paid his fare, and sat in the front half of the bus. The bus driver told him he had to move to the back of the bus. Uncle Lester refused to move. He told the bus driver that he had paid his fair, he was not moving and when the bus got to Bluefield, he would be on it.

The HUB Restaurant

Dad and a number of black men in Union Hall: carpooled together to work at Basset Furniture Company in Bassett, Virginia. Many times, they would stop at The HUB restaurant, a local restaurant in Rocky Mount. The restaurant was a "Whites Only Restaurant" which means they only served whites in the dining room. They would take black folks money, but the blacks had to go around to the back and order their food to go. When the men stopped to eat at the HUB, my Dad remained in the car waiting on them.

During one of those stops, Dad became angry at the very thought of being treated like a second-class citizen. A cab pulled up and Dad asked the cab driver if he had a fare and the man said no. Daddy told the cab driver to take him to Union Hall! He would rather spend the money to go back home than sit around waiting for his friends to get a meal, served around back because of the color of their skin.

North Carolina: Black and white students had to use separate sets of textbooks.

Florida: Not only did black and white students use separate textbooks, but the books had to be stored separately.

Unwritten rules barred blacks from white jobs in New York and kept them out of white stores in Los Angeles. Humiliation was about the best treatment blacks who broke such rules could hope for or expect.

Some of the Jim Crow laws still existed on the books well into the 21st century. For instance, today Virginia's Constitution permanently disenfranchises citizens with past felony convictions the right to vote. This impacted approximately 25% of the African American vote in Virginia during the 2008 presidential election. This law was established in the Virginia Constitutional Convention in 1902.

The Plan

"The original purpose of the law was plainly stated by Delegate Carter Glass at the Virginia Constitutional Convention of 1902. "This plan," Carter Glass said, "will eliminate the darkey as a political factor in this state in less than five years, so that no single county...will there be the least concern felt for the complete supremacy of the white race in the affairs of government."

The Jim Crow law debates and confederate statue dedications plainly spelled out the purpose for the laws and the statues.

This sets the backdrop and/or environment which my dad was born into and lived.

Racism from the Top

DAD WAS BORN on November 20, 1912, less than 50 years after The Civil War and less than 35 years after Reconstruction. As I mentioned in a previous chapter, Jim Crow, sharecropping, and the Ku Klux Klan (KKK) were alive, well and deeply entrenched into the fabric of American society—the law included.

He was the youngest one of four children: his sister Betty was four years older than him, and his brother Lester (pronounced Luster) was two years older than him. He also had a sister who died at birth, Willie Kate. Daddy was named after both his paternal and maternal grandfathers: Charles and Abron, and he was very proud to carry their names. His father's name was Edmond King Edwards. Isabel Wilkerson, author of *The Warmth of Other Suns* says black parents named their children names such as "King" because they were called by their given names and not their surnames. This allowed them to be called "King" and more importantly told them they were of kings.

Mar Smith and the Rabbit

Once when Dad was a boy, he was out hunting on his kinfolks place, the Russells. Just as Mr. Mar Smith walked up, Dad shot a rabbit. Mar said "We don't low no hunting on our place." Dad said, "We weren't hunting on your place, the dog jumped the rabbit on the Russell place, then it ran on your place and then back on the Russell place where I shot it."

At a corn shucking later that week, Mar said, "I started to smack one of Edmond's boys the other day, he sassed me." Dad replied, "No you didn't, and you won't smack'em now!"

My grandfather and Uncle Lester continued to travel to West Virginia in the winter to work in the coal mines. They left Dad behind to care for the farm and his mother. When they returned home, Uncle Lester would always have money and new suits. Dad said when he turned 18 and his dad and Uncle Lester started packing their bags to go to West Virginia, he packed his bags too.

When they went to West Virginia they would stay at a boarding house. At the boarding house they would receive a room to sleep in, along with a place to bathe, breakfast in the morning and a packed lunch. Dad took more after his mother's family and was larger than his dad and brother and needed more to eat than what was provided. His nick name in the mines was "Heavy." He was a strong, solidly built man. He said he was so hungry after breakfast and before lunch, he had eaten his lunch prior to lunch time and his dad and brother had to share their lunch with him.

I recall him mentioning that President Woodrow Wilson, a Virginian, and past New Jersey Governor who served as President from 1913 to 1921 was a racist and segregationist. It's amazing how Dad, even at a young age, noticed the mistreatment of his people. One of the stories he mentioned was about William Trotter, a civil rights leader who met with President Wilson on at least two occasions regarding the increasing number of government offices that was separating the workers based on race.

According to my research, The U.S. Treasury and Interior Department had separate toilets which President Wilson defended. In 1914, Mr. Trotter and his delegation which included Ida B. Wells presented Wilson with 20,000 signatures from thirty-eight states. They cited the on-the-job race separation—at eating tables, dressing rooms, restrooms, lockers and public toilets in government buildings. Trotter also cited the same discriminatory practices in other government departments: The Treasury Department, Bureau of Engraving and Printing, The Department of the Navy, The Interior Department, the Marine Hospital, and the War Department. He noted the support he and the Civil Rights community had provided to get Wilson elected. The meeting terminated when the president supported the surge in segregation and had Trotter and the entire delegation thrown out of the Oval Office.

Later in 1915, President Woodrow Wilson helped breathe new life into the KKK by showing the film "Birth of a Nation" at the White House.

The Birth of a Nation

The Birth of a Nation (originally called The Clansman) is a 1915 American silent epic drama film directed and co-produced by D. W. Griffith and starring Lillian Gish. The screenplay is adapted from the novel and play The Clansman, both by Thomas Dixon Jr., as well as Dixon's novel The Leopard's Spots. Griffith co-

wrote the screenplay with Frank E. Woods and co-produced the film with Harry Aitken. It was released on February 8, 1915.

The film is three hours long and was originally presented in two parts separated by an intermission; it was the first 12-reel film in the United States. The film chronicles the relationship of two families in the American Civil War and Reconstruction Era over the course of several years: the pro-Union Northern Stonemans and the pro-Confederacy Southern Camerons. The assassination of Abraham Lincoln by John Wilkes Booth is dramatized.

The film was a commercial success, though it was highly controversial for its portrayal of black men (many played by white actors in blackface) as unintelligent and sexually aggressive towards white women, and the portrayal of the Ku Klux Klan (KKK) as a heroic force. There were widespread black protests against The Birth of a Nation, such as in Boston, while thousands of white Bostonians flocked to see the film. The NAACP spearheaded an unsuccessful campaign to ban the film. Griffith's indignation at efforts to censor or ban the film motivated him to produce Intolerance the following year.

The film's release is also credited as being one of the events that inspired the formation of the "second era" Ku Klux Klan at Stone Mountain, Georgia the same year; it was used as a recruiting tool for the KKK, along with the trial and lynching of Leo Frank for the 1913 murder of Mary Phagan in Atlanta."

Wilson commented it was one of the best films ever written. After the film's release, there was an increase in lynching and other travesties committed against blacks. Dad spoke of his uncle being the last man to be hung, by law, in Rocky Mount at the courthouse.

World War I took place between 1914 and 1918. More than 360,000 black men served in WWI. The country welcomed them home with major race riots, the most serious in Chicago.

Eugene Williams' Drowning

"On July 27, 1919, a 17-year-old African-American boy named Eugene Williams was swimming with friends in Lake Michigan when he crossed the unofficial barrier (located at 29th Street) between the city's "white" and "black" beaches. A group of white men threw stones at Williams, hitting him, and he drowned. When police officers arrived on the scene, they refused to arrest the white man whom black eyewitnesses pointed to as the responsible party. Angry crowds began to gather on the beach, and reports of the incident—many distorted or exaggerated—spread quickly.

Violence soon broke out between gangs and mobs of black and white, concentrated in the South Side neighborhood surrounding the stockyards. After police were unable to quell the riots, the state militia was called in on the fourth day, but the fighting continued until August 3. Shootings, beatings and arson attacks eventually left 15 whites and 23 blacks dead,

and more than 500 more people (around 60 per-
cent black) injured. An additional 1,000 black
families were left homeless after rioters torched
their residences.

White mobs lynched veterans in uniform and
black Americans fought back. The National As-
sociation for the Advancement of Colored People
and the Urban League publicized abuses and
worked for redress. Government offices in
Washington D.C. were segregated. The tone of
the country was set from the White House.

The *New York Times* front-page story was
headlined, "President Resents Negro's Criticism"
while the front-page headline in the *New York
Press* read: "Wilson Rebukes Negro Who 'Talks
Up' to Him."

Such disfranchising laws included poll taxes,
literacy tests, vouchers of "good character," and
disqualification for "crimes of moral turpitude."
These laws were "color-blind" on their face but
were designed to exclude black citizens disproportionately by allowing white election officials

to apply the procedures selectively. Other laws and practices, such as the "white primary," attempted to evade the 15th Amendment by allowing "private" political parties to conduct elections and establish qualifications for their members.

White Primaries

White primaries were primary elections held in the Southern United States in which only white voters were permitted to participate. White primaries were established by the state Democratic Party units or by state legislatures in many Southern states after 1890. The white primary was one method used by white Democrats to disenfranchise most black and other minority voters. They also passed laws and constitutions with provisions to raise barriers to voter registration, completing disenfranchisement from 1890 to 1908 in all states of the former Confederacy.

The Texas Legislature passed a law in 1923 that allowed political parties to make their own rules for their primaries. The dominant Democratic Party banned black and Mexican American minorities from participating. The Supreme Court, in 1927, 1932, and 1935, heard three Texas cases related to white primaries. In the 1927 and 1932 cases, the Supreme Court ruled in favor of the plaintiff, saying that state laws establishing a white primary violated the Fourteenth Amendment. Texas changed its law in response, delegating authority to political parties to establish their own rules for primaries. In Grovey v. Townsend (1935), the Supreme Court ruled that this practice was constitutional, as it was administered by the Democratic Party, which was a private, not a state institution.

In 1944, the Supreme Court ruled 8-1 against the Texas white primary system in Smith v. Allwright. In that case, the Court ruled that the 1923 Texas state law was unconstitutional, because it allowed the state Democratic Party to racially discriminate. After the case, most Southern states ended their selectively inclusive white primaries. They retained other devices of disenfranchisement, particularly in terms of barriers to voter registration, such as poll taxes and literacy tests. These generally survived legal challenges as they applied to all potential voters. But in practice they were administered in a discriminatory manner by white officials, that resulted in most blacks being excluded from the political system in the South until after the 1960s, no matter their level of education or property ownership.

While much of the disfranchisement started in earnest when Dad was a child, it had a far-reaching effect on him as an adult. In fact, because of intimidation, violence, and racial discrimination in State voting laws, a mere three percent of voting-age black men and women were registered to vote in 1940, when Dad was 28 years of age. Attempts to change voting laws were met with animosity and outright violence, yet my parents were instrumental in making sure blacks in the area were registered to vote. Dad read the Pittsburg Courier and the Chicago Defender (both African American newspapers) to keep up with the political activities around the country.

The county seat and courthouse are in Rocky Mount, Virginia which is in the center of the county. However, during the early years, the county held court and court activities in the different communities/districts at country stores and/or churches. Court was held at these places along with court activities such as paying your taxes.

The Voter Registration Story

When Daddy and Mama moved to Union Hall, he went to the courthouse in Union Hall to register to vote. They told him that he had to go to Rocky Mount to register, so he went to Rocky Mount to register. The people in Rocky Mount told him he had to register in Union Hall.

He told them, if he could not register to vote, he was not going to pay his land taxes (head tax or capitation tax). They told him to go back to Union Hall and they were sure he could register. He went back to Union Hall where they finally allowed him to register.

Once he registered, Mama registered as well. At that time the only Blacks registered to vote were three black men in Union Hall. These men worked on the farm of the people that did the registration.

Fueled by his need to make a difference, Dad and Mama then set out and registered other blacks in the County. My parents helped scores of people register to vote!

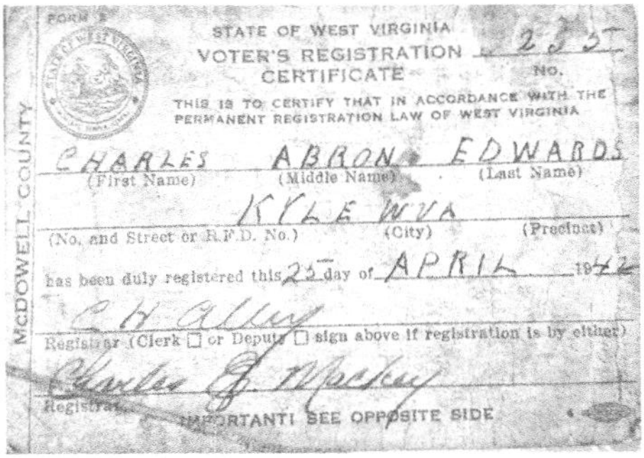

STATE OF WEST VIRGINIA
VOTER'S REGISTRATION CERTIFICATE No. 235
THIS IS TO CERTIFY THAT IN ACCORDANCE WITH THE PERMANENT REGISTRATION LAW OF WEST VIRGINIA

CHARLES ABRON EDWARDS
(First Name) (Middle Name) (Last Name)

KYLE WVA
(No. and Street or R.F.D. No.) (City) (Precinct)

has been duly registered this 25 day of APRIL 1942

Registrar (Clerk ☐ or Deputy ☐ sign above if registration is by either)

Registrar

IMPORTANT! SEE OPPOSITE SIDE

McDOWELL COUNTY

Dad's Voter Registration Card, 1942

CHAPTER 6

Separate and Unequal

IN 1896 THE U.S. Supreme Court heard the case Plessy vs. Ferguson and upheld "separate but equal" which became the law of the land in the South. In the South public facilities had to have separate facilities for blacks and whites.

Black men could not expect and did not get equal protection under the law. They were lynched, cheated out of money and land with no recourse, and their wives, mothers, and daughters continued to be raped with no protection from the law.

Not Entitled to Freedom

"In the decades after the violent suppression of Reconstruction, opinion leaders nurtured a simmering rage directed at African Americans' sense of entitlement to their freedom. Ida B. Wells estimated in the 1890s that 10,000 lynchings had occurred in the first 30 years after the Civil War. The great bulk of these were the result of white night riders, Klux Klan terror, and election violence in the years up to 1877. Then the killings settled into a pattern of roughly 100 people a year murdered by white vigilante violence over the next 50 years. This record translates to one person killed every three and a half days for assault, murder, and rape—as well as for "wanting a drink of water" "sassing a white lady," "being troublesome," or for "nothing."

According to a 2016 article published in *The New Republic*, entitled *How the Klan Got Its Hood* author Alison Kinney writes:

How the Klan Got Its Hood

"Starting in the 1880s, spectacle lynchings attracted crowds of up to <u>15,000 white</u> participant-witnesses, who booked special <u>excursion trains to reach lynching sites</u>. They snatched victims' clothing, bone fragments, and organs as souvenirs; they photographed themselves, smiling, posing with their kids beside the broken, burned bodies of their victims; they scrapbooked the photos and mailed them as postcards, confident that they'd never be held accountable for their terrorism. They didn't wear hoods, because they didn't need to.

Lynchings were not spontaneous outbursts of "mob" violence, but the predictable result of institutional support and the outright participation of political elites. The lynchers of Leo Frank, in Marietta, Georgia in 1915, included a former governor, judge, mayor and state legislator, sheriff, county prosecutor, lawyer and banker, business owner, U.S. senator's son, and the founders of the Marietta Country Club.

Frank's atypical case—he was white and Jew-ish—attracted media attention that thousands of black victims never received, yet it exposed the ways that elites and authorities exonerated themselves by blaming mob violence on so-called "crackers." Meanwhile, Mississippi gov-ernor, later U.S. senator James K. Vardaman said in 1907, "If it is necessary every Negro in the state will be lynched; it will be done to main-tain white supremacy."

During this dark period in America's history, it would be pure folly to "sass" or to do *anything* that could be construed as "disrespecting" a white person. However, in Dad and Uncle Lester's view it was pure folly not to address a white person who was disrespecting them!

Them Edwards Boys and The Union Hall Scuffle

Dad and Uncle Lester were close in age and looked very much alike. They visited Union Hall often from West Virginia. Once Daddy and Uncle

Lester were in town for the weekend from West Virginia visiting their mom and dad. Dad and Uncle Lester use to buy cars together. They even shared the same driver's license. During one visit, the four of them: Dad, Uncle Lester, Grandma and Grandpa decided to visit their Grandma's sister, Aunt Rossie. On the way, they stopped at the local store to purchase Grandpa some cigars. Three white men pulled in behind them on the other side of the pump and started blowing their horn.

"Get that dang thing out of the way before I shoot a hole through it."

Dad jumped out of the car, "Man you don't know who the hell you talking to.

Grandma said, "Charles that might be the law." Dad said, "The law ain't acting that stupid."

One of the white men and Daddy met. Daddy socked him and knocked him down and Grandpa jumped on him. Daddy started fighting the next man. The last man started to open the *rumble in the back. Uncle Lester said, "Man, you better let that damn thing down, don't come outta there with nothing." The man let it back down.*

The next time Daddy and Uncle Lester were in town, a friend said when the men, who were visiting from Louisiana, got to the ranch they said they ran into the damndest niggers they had ever seen driving a grey Chevrolet with West Virginia tags. The friend said, "Charles and Lester Edwards got hold a yall's ass."

Grandpa's Watch

Grandpa and his brother Henry both had a watch in the jewelry store for repair. My grandmother had been to the jeweler several times to pick up the watches, but the jeweler could not find the watches because they had had a fire. So, Dad went with her to the store so that she could describe Grandpa's watch. She told the jeweler that Grandpa's watch had a dent in it. The jeweler became angry and said Grandma was sassing him. Dad said, "How the hell is she gone sass you and she is old as you are?" The jeweler turned red, went in the back of the store and came out with both watches.

These ole pecks use to be something!

CHAPTER 7

Went In Coming Out

MOM AND DAD met in West Virginia. They were married on November 25, 1936 in Welch, West Virginia (McDowell County) by Reverend W. A. Pittman.

Helen Marie Holliday, my mom, was born in Thorpe, West Virginia. She was one of six children and Dad was seven years her elder. He says he saw her for the first time when she was being baptized in an outdoor pond. Her father was a local coal miner and he and Dad worked and socialized together.

They settled in West Virginia where they enjoyed living despite the prevalence of racism and injustice. There was a viable black community of doctors, teachers and businesspersons. My parents moved from coal mining town to coal mining town as Dad worked in various coal mines. They bought tailored clothes, and both were spiffy dressers. When they would visit Virginia, they were the buzz of the community because of the way they dressed and the cars they drove.

When they moved to a coal mining town, they lived in the coal mining housing. They shopped at the coal mining stores. Dad's records show he worked in the following mines as a coal loader from 1930 to 1947:

Company	Town	Year
Winding Gulf Co. No. 2	Winding Gulf	1930 – 1935
U.S. Steel Coal & Coke	Gary	1935 – 1936
Coal Wood Mining	Coal Wood	1937
U.S. Steel Coal & Coke	Gary	1937 – 1938
Jones Coal & Coke Co.	Jenkins	1938

Carper Coal Company	Stanford	1938-1939
Lillybrook Coal Company	Kallanie	1939 - 1940
Algoma Coal and Coke	Algoma	1940 - 1941
Lake Superior	Lake Superior	1941 - 1945
Race Coal and Coke	Keystone	1945 - 1947

He told us stories of the bosses in the mines that use to make the rounds during voting time telling their employers how to vote, which Dad ignored. In one disagreement with a mining boss, Dad told the man, "I was looking for a job when I came here, and I will be looking for a job when I leave." In a discussion with another person, Dad expressed that he was in the coal mining business to make money for a short while. He did not plan to make it a living. The gentlemen told him, once a coal miner, always a coal miner. Dad replied, "I went in coming out!"

The coal mining work was dirty, difficult and dangerous. He told us of how he was lowered deep into the mines 20 and 30 feet deep and worked on his hands and knees for the bulk of the day. He suffered one accident that cost him half of his left-hand index finger up to his knuckle. He was treated by the company doctor and sent to Raleigh General Hospital in Beckley West Virginia.

Their little family expanded, and Charles Jr. was born in 1937; Gloria Marie was born in 1939; and Evelyn Marlene came along in 1941.

Charles Jr. was born premature, yet when it was time for him to enter into the school system, my parents sent him on time. They decided to send Gloria Marie to school two years early to be with Charles Jr. Initially, Charles Jr. and Gloria Marie attended school in Kyle. Later, they attended school in Mayberry.

Dad and Uncle Lester owned and managed a colored baseball team. They worked hard in the mines during the week and traveled with the baseball team (with family in tow) on the weekends. After the games they would meet at the different homes and play cards while the children played in another room. The most popular card game was 5-Up.

On August 30, 1943, Dad purchased 46 acres of land in Union Hall, VA for $1600.00, $250.00 of which was cash in hand paid and the remainder of $1350.00 as evidenced by note. After Charles Jr. and Gloria Marie attended school in West Virginia for a couple of years, my parents sent them to live with Dad's parents in Virginia and they attended Ephesus, the local colored one room schoolhouse.

Dad had also asked his dad to keep an eye on a little white house and three acres of land on the main thoroughfare of Union Hall owned by Dad's cousin, who was the daughter of his aunt and uncle. His mom's sister married his Dad's brother (Roxie Mattox Edwards and Henry Edwards). Both had passed by this time and left their property to their daughter.

In 1944 there was a forced land sale of the property. Dad's dad purchased the house and land for $2,250.00. The purchase is recorded in the courthouse as such: *This deed made and entered into this the 24th day of July 1944 by and between Clyde H. Perdue, Special Commissioner as herein afterward, party of the first part, and Edmund K. Edwards party of the second part."*

World War II took place between 1939 to 1945. There were many changes for Blacks due to WWII, because of the link between Hitler's "master race" and America's Jim Crow (white supremacy).

The Master Race

The master race. . . is a concept in Nazi and Neo-Nazi ideology in which the Nordic or Aryan races, predominant among Germans and other northern European peoples, are deemed the highest in racial hierarchy. Members of this alleged master race were referred to as Herrenmenschen ("master humans").

The United Nations was shocked and appalled by the Jim Crow system of the South.

During this time Dad and Mama were making the trips back and forth to West Virginia. Dad, always a great provider, made sure that Mama had whatever she needed to take care of our family. He would not tolerate her being disrespected because of the color of her skin.

Mick or Mack

Mom and Dad were coming in from West Virginia and were tired. They stopped at the Mick or Mack to buy some chickens, so they would not have to kill and dress chickens so they could eat when they got home. The butcher prepared a couple of chickens for them and Mom and Dad had the chickens in their basket. My mom then saw a steak she wanted. Dad ask the butcher for a steak. The butcher reached for a dark dried up looking steak. Mom says, "Oh no, I don't want that one. I want that one" and pointed to a nice red steak. The butcher said, "If you don't want this one, then you don't want none." Dad threw the chickens back up on the counter and said, "No, we don't, and we don't want the damn chickens either." Mom and Dad then walked out of the store and continued home.

CHAPTER 8

Life in Virginia

MY BROTHER, TERRANCE Eugene was born in 1946. Two years later my parents moved to Virginia where they had the remainder of their children.

Initially, they moved in with Dad's parents. Court records show that on January 1, 1949 Mom and Dad purchased their first home from Dad's parents with money left to Mama from her father for the same $2,250.00 that Grandpa purchased the land for in 1944 on behalf of Dad. *"This deed made and entered into this the 10th day of January in the year 1949, by and between Edmund K. Edwards, and Sallie Mattox Edwards, his wife, parties of the first part, and Charles Abron Edwards, their son, all members of the colored race, party of the second part."*

The house was a small white clapboard house on three acres of land encircled by the main thoroughfare of Franklin County, Route 40, now named Old Franklin Turnpike and a dirt State Road 662, now paved and named Edwardsway Road. The front of the house faced Route 40 and the back faced Route 662. Because of how the house was situated between these two roads, the main door utilized in the house was the back door which faced route 662. There was an oak tree, two apple trees, one stark delicious and one green apple tree, a pear tree, a peach tree, a cherry tree, along with a switch bush in the backyard.

The house had four rooms. The back-door entrance opened into the kitchen. It served as the main entrance into our home. The stove was an old-fashioned stove where you had to lift the burners to place the wood which provided the fire/heat for cooking. So many meals of love were prepared in this kitchen along with milk churned to make buttermilk and butter. Evening baths were taken in tin tubs in the kitchen by the stove for heat. From the kitchen was the entrance to Mom and Dad's bedroom. This was the center of the house which also had a door to the outside. It was not only the center of the house because of its location, it was the center of activity.

The next room was the living room which had an exit door to the front porch and a door that led to the back room which served as a bedroom for the children. In 1949 when the home was purchased my parents had four children. This small clapboard house would see a lot of activity. Children came and went and returned with spouses and more children and left again. There was an outdoor old-fashioned well right outside the kitchen door which contained a bucket and rope. Dad built a room that encircled the well so that the family did not have to go outside to get water. Naturally this room was called the well room.

He also built a back porch. Now the entrance from the back yard was onto the back porch and then into the well room. Later he put a pump on the well and the water was pumped out of the well. It was much like a large modern-day mud room. It also contained a roll around old-fashioned wringer washer.

All the rooms were heated with their own small wood burning stoves for heat. It was warmly furnished and heavily utilized. There was no in-door bathroom; however, the out-house was close by.

Ephesus Primitive Baptist Church was across Route 662 and our grandparents and many of the African American residents of Union Hall belonged to the church. The best times were the annual "Sosations," that is Associations. People would come from all over and have church for days. There was always plenty of food, singing and merriment to go around. My grandmother was the "Mother" of the church and my grandfather served as a deacon.

My parents also owned 20 acres beside the church across from our house which they purchased from Dad's sister, Betty. Aunt Betty and her husband, Wayman Law, lived on the other side of the church. All the land around us was owned by our family except for the church, and the church was family. The land that Aunt Betty owned across the road from us was 25 acres and connected to Grandpa's 100-acre farm.

As previously mentioned, Ephesus School was yards away from my parents' home across from Ephesus Church. It was a Rosenwald School built by my grandfather and local men. It had a pot-belly stove. The teachers boarded with my grandparents and would travel home on the weekends. Some of the teachers lived as far away as West Virginia. Charles Jr and Gloria Marie attended Ephesus until 6th grade and then transferred to Franklin County Training School which later became L. M. Waid School in Rocky Mount which was also built with Rosenwald funds. L. M. Waid School was 1st through 12th grade for colored children.

Rosenwald Schools

Julius Rosenwald, part owner and leader of Sears, Roebuck and Company, collaborated with Booker T. Washington to provide funds for what is commonly known as Rosenwald schools. Mr. Rosenwald working with Mr. Washington donated millions of dollars to build schools primarily for the education of African American children in the rural south. This was specifically special to Franklin County since Booker T. Washington is a native of Franklin County where he was born into slavery and freed by the Civil War and amendments at the age of 9. He notes in his book *Up From Slavery* he, his family, and the other enslaved persons on the large farm learned of their freedom from a Union soldier who read from a General Order. This farm was only 16 miles from where my great-grandparents were enslaved.

My parents and other black parents around the county chose to send their grade school children to L. M. Waid prior to 8th grade rather than the local one room schools. L. M. Waid School had better facilities and separate classrooms based on grades versus the one room schoolhouses around the county. My siblings in grade school also attended L. M. Waid. Essentially, you had black grade school children in the County going to one room schools around the county and some of them attending grade school in Rocky Mount at L.M Waid. Clearly, the school district did not care where the black children went to school, as long as they were not going to school with the white children.

Our family continued to grow: Linda Carol in 1949, Ruby Nadean in 1951, Janis Faye in 1953 and Crystal Diane in 1955.

During this time, most black people's babies were delivered at home by a midwife. In 1953 when Janis Faye was born, Mama delivered in the Rocky Mount Hospital. However, Dad did not like the way Mama was treated so the next child, Crystal Diane, was born at home.

On March 5, 1954 Dad purchased 40 acres of my Granddad's 100-acre farm for $2000.00 cash in hand. It is separated by the creek that runs through the property.

Charles Jr. and Gloria Marie graduated Franklin County Normal School in 1955. Initially Charles Jr. went to Cleveland, Ohio and lived with Uncle Lester and Aunt Eva, before returning back to Union Hall where he worked and raised his family. Gloria Marie entered Virginia Union College in Richmond, Virginia.

Clayton's

My sister Ruby had a speech impediment. So, at the age of 5, my parents sent her to Ephesus to help her with her impediment.

The teacher decided to take the students on a field trip (walking) one day to a local gas station/country store, Clayton's, about half a mile from our house. At that time all of the local stores were called by the owner's first name. In Union Hall there was Clayton's, Pasley's, Harry's and Joe Billy's. Clayton's was only a half mile from our home, the other three were about a mile from our home. Clayton's was Jim Crow. They had signs for entry into the store that read White and Colored. Therefore, my parents did not frequent that store and did not allow us to frequent the store.

The teacher and students had to pass by our house to make it to Clayton's. Dad happened to be in the back yard. Of course, he asked them where they were headed. The teacher informed him they were taking a field trip and walking to Clayton's. He explained that Ruby was not allowed to go to that store and why, and that she could stay there at the house until they returned. When the class returned, Ruby was allowed to go back to school. The teacher bought Ruby candy.

During that same year, President Harry Truman took decisive action to promote racial equality. He urged Congress to abolish the poll tax, enforce fair voting and hiring practices, and end Jim Crow transportation between states. Four Southern states abandoned Truman's Democratic Party in protest. Then, as Commander in Chief, Truman ordered the complete integration of the Armed Forces. He did not wipe out racism, but trained to obey commands, officers complied as best they could. In Korea, during the 1950s, integrated U.S. forces fought their first war.

Dad was always proud to say that none of his children were afraid of work and all believed they are equal to any and everybody. Even though my parents had very little education themselves, they believed education was the great equalizer and stressed and ensured all of their children obtained an education to the best of their abilities.

We saw our father as an enigma. Outside of the home he was a man among men; he was a man of honor and integrity. At home he was a man before his time. He was our biggest cheerleader, and he did not believe in corporal punishment. One of my fondest memories is about the time he "whipped" my sisters.

The Necktie

It was a typical winter night that Linda, Ruby, Faye and Diane were in the bedroom readying for bed. It was a large room with two sets of bunkbeds. The winters in Franklin County in the 50s were very cold. Therefore, each of their beds were complete with very heavy homemade quilts. Either quilted by My mom or grandma.

Linda, Ruby, Faye and Diane instead of being snuggled in their beds as they were supposed to be, were playing, laughing, giggling, and jumping from bed to bed.

Mom and Dad were in their room which was two rooms down from my sisters.

Mom hollered back and told them to quieten down and go to bed. They continued to play. Mom hollered back a second time and told them to quiet down and go to bed. They continued to play. Dad then hollered back and told them to quieten down and go to bed. When moms speak, we think about it. When dads speak, we ask how high. They continued to play. Dad grabbed one of his neck ties and headed for the backroom. The girls, hearing his footsteps, jumped in bed under their heavy winter quilts.

He entered their room and found them in their beds under the winter cover. He had to act since he had to come to the room, so he then proceeded to whip them with his necktie while they were under their winter quilts.

As you've guessed by now, Dad did not whip his children and did not allow anyone else to do so, other than my mom—because he had no choice—but no one else, not our grandparents, aunts or uncles. He believed whipping children made them mean and that most people did not know how to whip children. And if you were going to whip children it should never be done in anger.

My father was a gentle man. If you needed someone to comb your hair softly, he was your man. Even though many times he would arrive home late after we had already eaten dinner, there was nothing like getting something off his plate and he always had that pack of juicy fruit gum in his left shirt pocket.

Despite his gentle ways and protective manner, he believed in doing and not just talking. He set a standard and instituted integration in as many ways as he could.

Integrating at the Wheat Thrashing

In the 1940s and 1950s Dad and Grandpa worked closely together day to day working on their farms. Annually a number of farmers both black and white in the community worked together to thrash each other's wheat. This allowed them to utilize the equipment owned by a couple of them and provided the manpower each farmer needed without having to hire the manpower required to thrash the wheat.

The couple of white men that owned the equipment set the round robin schedule of going from farm to farm to thrash each farmer's wheat.

The farmer's wife whose farm they worked each day was responsible for preparing the lunch for all the farmers.

The men would start the wheat thrashing early in the morning, break for lunch and then continue to work after lunch.

Both Dad and Grandpa participated in the workings.

Of course, during this time in the South, the Jim Crow laws did not allow blacks and whites to eat in restaurants together and this mindset spilled over into noncommercial environments. When the farmers came in for lunch the white farmers ate first. Once the white farmers finished eating, the black farmers were allowed to eat. This was true in both the black and white farmers' homes.

Dad talked with all the Black farmers and told them it was ridiculous for them to allow the white men to go into their homes and eat at their tables before they ate. Dad let them know when they got to his house that year all of the farmers were going to eat at the same time. All the Black farmers were in agreement. When they got to Dad's farm, he had everybody eat at the same time. Dad had an older black farmer set at the head of the table and "turn" the grace. He then winked his eye at Daddy.

Everything went smoothly as planned. Once the farmers finished eating, they returned to work and completed the round robin style of visiting the farms.

The following year all the farmers got back together to thrash wheat. When it came close to our farm they had not announced whose farm they were going to next, so Dad asked if they were going to his farm next or another black farmer. They always needed a little advanced notice; so that the wives could plan to prepare the lunch.

The first man Dad ask said the other white man was in charge and for Dad to ask him. Dad approached and asked him. The man replied,

"Well Charles, I don't think we are gon' thrash your wheat this year. Last year when we went to your house you feed the black and white together." Dad then said, "If all I ever lose is a field of wheat, I'll be a rich man." He then threw his pitchfork down and walked off. Grandpa threw his pitchfork down and followed.

All the other farmers stayed and continued the round robin farm visits along with lunch as they had been doing in the past.

Because white supremacy still reigned and white men were still able to abuse black men, women and children at will and did, Dad did not allow his wife or children to work on white men's farms. We worked hard on our own farm but did not hire out to other farms.

I'll Treat 'Em Good and Feed 'Em

Once Dad was in the yard and a white man saw him as he was driving by and told him if he let his wife and kids come work for him, he would "treat'em good, feed'em good, pay'em and bring'em back." Dad's response to the man was if he allowed his wife and kids come and work for him, he would treat'em good, feed'em good, pay'em and bring'em home. The man's face turned a bright crimson red and he drove off.

Charles was never a man to take the path of least resistance, instead he took the path that God defined for man as being made in His own image.

One of the biggest disagreements Mom and Dad had was about her employment. He worked as a janitor at a huge Methodist Church in Rocky Mount. The Methodist tradition is to change their ministers after so many years. Mom went to work in the home of a white minister, and this was a huge issue for Dad. She wanted to work there because we needed the money and she knew she could handle herself. Dad did not want her to work there because during this time it was well known in the black community that black women that worked as domestic servants in white people's homes were mistreated. The white men in the homes sexually abused the black women that worked in their home. Based on the laws and practices it was very difficult for their husbands to do anything about it. However, Dad knew that if something happened, he would have to retaliate and take care of business. He did not want to end up in jail.

Evelyn Marlene and Terrance Eugene graduated from Lee M. Wade School in 1958 and 1964 respectively. Evelyn Marlene entered Apex Beauty School in Richmond, Virginia and Terrance Eugene married and moved into a house owned by Dad on the 47 acres he had bought previously. Grandpa Edmond King (Dad's father) passed away June 1960.

Penny Adriane was born 1959 and Ronald Brent was born in 1965. By this time things were a little better. Both Penny and Ronnie were born in the Rocky Mount Hospital.

He always believed his children deserved the very best and was never afraid to take the lonely road to make certain the best was made available to them regardless of the obstacles faced and the consequences endured. In addition, he understood that integration of the schools was an important step and sacrifice that he, Mom and his children had to make for future generations.

CHAPTER 9

Education: Freedom of Choice

THE SUPREME COURT'S landmark decision of *Brown v. Board of Education* (1954) regarding racial segregation overturned the 1896 Supreme Court decision *Plessy v. Ferguson.*

Around the country there were several black parents suing local school districts in order to provide their children better classrooms, books, etc.

The Right to Fairness

After seeking legal advice from NAACP lawyers in March 1951, a group of parents asked the school board to admit their children to Claymont High. When the State Board of Education refused, the parents sued the state of Delaware. The court case was filed in August 1951 as Belton v. Gebhart (a member of the State Board of Education). A second case, Bulah v. Gebhart, was brought by Sarah Bulah, a parent who had made several attempts to convince the Delaware Department of Public Instruction to provide bus transportation for black children in the town of Hockessin. Particularly galling was the fact that a bus for white children passed her house twice a day, but would not pick up her daughter. The Delaware court concluded that "the mental health problems created by racial segregation attributed to a lack of educational progress, and furthermore that under the separate but equal doctrine the plaintiffs had a right to send their children to the white schools." This was the first time in the United States that a white high school and elementary school were ordered to admit black children. The State Attorney General immediately filed an appeal. On August 28, 1952, the Supreme Court of Delaware upheld the decision. In late November, the State Attorney General filed a petition for the U.S. Supreme Court to review the case.

In three of the four cases the Federal Courts upheld segregation. In the case mentioned above, the parents appealed and won, so the district appealed the decision.

Consequently, The Supreme Court agreed to hear four cases in combination, grouped as *Brown v. Board of Education.* The four cases were comprised of Oliver Brown, et. al from Topeka Kansas, Delaware, South Carolina and Virginia.

The Virginia plaintiff, ironically, was from Prince Edward County, Virginia which borders Appomattox, Virginia where Lee surrendered to Grant. In Prince Edward County, Barbra Johns, a

16-year-old student led a protest to walk out of the "black high school."

On May 17, 1954, at noon, the Supreme Court announced their unanimous decision that racial segregation of children in public schools, even in schools of equal quality, hurt minority children. They wrote, "Separate educational facilities are inherently unequal." The practice violates the Constitution's 14th amendment and must stop.

The trend of increasing racial and economic segregation was a nationwide trend—not just in Alabama and other Southern states. The South, however, was the only region in the country to see a net increase in private school enrollment between 1960 and 2000. Historically, where private school enrollment is higher, support for spending in public schools tends to be lower.

Dad worked as a janitor for several years at Franklin County High School, the local white high school. This job allowed him to see, daily, that the all black school system in the county— the one his children attended—was separate, but certainly not equal.

In Prince Edward County, Virginia, County officials shut down all the public schools from 1959 to 1965 rather than integrate. This was part of Virginia's "massive resistance," led by Virginia Senator Harry Byrd.

"Massive resistance" was a movement against federally mandated integration in the public-school system and the birth of private school vouchers and school choice. The state legislature passed a law which allowed local government entities to revoke funds from and shut down districts and schools. Schools were also closed in Charlottesville and Norfolk.

Prince Edward County closed the doors to all their public schools. Once they shut down the public schools, they then used tax dollars to give vouchers to white students to attend private schools. Many black students moved away for education, while others dropped out of the education system all together. Today, the Prince Edward Public School System is still majority black; however, the county population is majority white.

In a last-ditch effort to stave off integration and show separate but equal, Franklin County's school board took three decisive actions:

1. On December 1, 1957 they renamed the Franklin County Trade School (built in 1920 from Rosenwald funds in Rocky Mount for the black children in Franklin County) to L. M. Waid School. Along with providing a new building for the students, the trade school remained 1st through 12th grade and now L. M. Waid School went from 1st through 12th grade. Blacks in Franklin County graduating from the 12th grade still did not graduate from a "high school."

They opened the doors to two brand new elementary schools in the County to get the black children in the County out of one room schoolhouses into brick elementary schools with actual classrooms separated by grade level.

2. On the north side of the county was Booker T. Washington Elementary School built alongside Booker T. Washington National Monument. The school was built on land donated by Sidney J. Phillips and the Booker T. Washington Memorial. The county consolidated six one-room schools into Booker T. Elementary. It operated from 1954 to 1966. The school only had one principal during that span who served as a principal, a teacher, bus driver, janitor and as a ranger at Booker T. Washington National Monument. The building had separate classrooms for the different grades. There was no eat-in cafeteria. The students passed through the cafeteria, picked up their lunch and ate in the classroom. Once the doors closed in 1966, the school was donated back to the National Park Service. It has been in the Park's plans since 1974 to turn the building into an educational center. Currently, it houses the staff of the monument versus part of

the historical story or an educational center.

3. On the south side of the county Truevine Elementary School was built in the Truevine community. The school was opened in the middle of the 1960–1961 school year and closed in 1970 when all the schools in Franklin County instituted forced integration. My grade school aged siblings transferred from L. M. Waid Elementary to Truevine Elementary: Linda, 6th grade; Ruby, 4th grade; and Faye, 2nd grade. The building most recently served as a factory, but for the past number of years has been empty.

Prior to Booker T. Washington Elementary and Truevine Elementary, there were a number of one room schools around the county where most of the black children in the county attended until 8th grade. One such school was Ephesus School in Union Hall built in 1925-26 at a cost of $2,350.

Even though, my siblings attended L. M. Waid, they participated in school programs at L. M. Waid, as well as Ephesus. They all started to school every year the first day of school and did not miss any days unless there was a serious illness. A number of children including those that were sharecroppers started school in October when the tobacco season lightened up. We worked our tobacco in the summer. When school started, we worked our tobacco on the weekends and after school.

"Freedom of Choice" came to Virginia in 1965, 11 years after the Supreme Court struck down "separate, but equal." This was after the Little Rock Nine in 1957. After mass resistance failed, Virginia implemented "freedom of choice." This allowed black families to choose to integrate into the white school system or remain in the black school system.

My parents were always very active in the PTO, and other school events in the schools, as were their children. There are the many stories of my older brothers and sisters playing baseball, basketball, in the band, in the choir, May Day Queens, etc.

By 1965 their oldest four children had graduated 12th grade (Franklin County Training School and L. M. Waid) and their youngest two children were not old enough to enter the school system. They had four daughters in the school system: Linda, Ruby, Faye and Diane who were going to the 11th, 9th, 7th, and 5th grades, respectively.

Dad and Mom sent their children that were still in the school system to the historically all white schools. They also visited other black parents in the County encouraging them to send their children to the "white school system." Some did, but most did not. This was a heavy decision for our parents. They knew they were sending their precious daughters into harm's way. However, they knew this had to be done for progress.

To achieve progress and protest educational injustice, my parents and sisters' school participation changed. My sisters went from being teachers' pets and May Day Queens to being subjected to racial slurs and unfair treatment by students, teachers, and administration. They had to fight a minimum of twice a day—each time they got on the school bus they had to fight to get a seat on the way to school and on the return ride home.

The Elementary School (Glade Hill Elementary) is two miles from our home which is where Faye and Diane attended. Glade Hill was built in 1935. Franklin County Junior High and Franklin County High was a 13-mile ride. Those were the schools Ruby and Linda attended, respectively. Linda and Ruby were responsible for getting themselves and the younger sisters' seats on the bus. As mentioned earlier, every day started with a fight because the students on the bus did not want any "niggers" sitting with them.

In their wisdom, my parents did not send them alone and their participation in the school system went from attending PTOs, planning programs, raising funds, attending programs and seeing their children play baseball, basketball, in the band and other programs to constantly talking with principals and superintendents about issues in the school system. This was a new phenomenon for my sisters and our parents.

Of course, the years just prior to 1965, the news was full of black's demonstrating and marching, along with whites bombing, water hosing and siccing dogs on the protesters. There were no National Guards to protect my sisters. My Dad gave them the talk. He expected them to go to school, do their work and be respectful and not to start any fights. However, he did not expect them to come home beaten up. If anyone hit them, he expected them to fight back and if one got in a fight, they were all to fight. Charles Jr. explained to them they could not fight like girls. They had to ball their fists up and punch the person in the gut.

On the first day of school, the four of them walked about a quarter of a mile to the bus stop. They were all afraid. To calm their nerves, they sang the new 1965 hit by the Temptations; "My Girl." Once they reached the bus stop, a bus full of white kids hanging out of the windows shouting "nigger," stopped. The bus driver asked them if this was their bus. They said no. The next bus that stopped also had kids hanging out the window hollering "nigger" and other racial epithets. However, this was their bus and they boarded.

Several incidents stand out in my mind: one where Dad insisted my sisters stand up to the bullying they had been enduring since attending the all-white school and the other where Dad let the bus driver know that he would not stand for his children to be harmed or mistreated.

Water Guns

My sisters informed our parents that daily the other kids on the bus had water guns and were constantly shooting them with water on their rides to and from school. Daily, even in the winter by the time they arrived at school or home, their heads were wet. They informed the principals, and our parents talked to the principals. The principals and superintendent said there was nothing they could do, because they could not determine who was shooting the water. Linda told Dad she had spotted this one girl shooting them with water.

To end this harassment, Dad instructed Linda and Ruby along with a friend of theirs to each take a gallon of water with them. He told them, "When you get off the bus, wait at the door and when the girl steps off that bus drench her with the water."

As always, the water shooting started. The three of them: Linda, Ruby and their friend sat quietly and endured the continued firing of water. Once the bus stopped at the high school to let them off, the three stepped off the bus and waited at the bus door. When the guilty party got off the bus that morning, the three of them threw their gallon of water on the girl.

When the friend threw the water, she dropped her jug. The glass broke and cut the girl on the leg. In addition, Ruby kicked the girl and left a nice pretty footprint on her beautiful yellow London fog coat.

Of course, now the principals were ready to act. Since Ruby attended Franklin County Junior High and Linda attended Franklin County High School, Dad had to deal with the principals of both schools.

When the Junior High principal called Dad, Ruby was sitting in his office. He shared with Dad what occurred, so Dad asked to speak with Ruby. He asked her if she was alright. Ruby said yes. Then Dad asked to speak with the principal. Ruby told us that while the principal was talking to Dad, she began to see red rising from his neck until his entire face was red.

The principals informed Dad they would have to suspend both Linda and Ruby for a couple of weeks.

Dad told the principals, "I agree that the girl who used the water gun on Linda, Ruby, and their friend should be suspended for the entire time for causing all of the issues on the bus for the past several months, which we have all been trying to get to the bottom of. However, since we

*have been reporting this issue for months and
no one was able to do anything about it and it is
one day before Christmas break, I will allow
Linda and Ruby to take a break for the one day.
However, they will be back in School when
school starts back after the Christmas holiday."*

*After the Christmas holiday, Linda and Ruby
returned to school and the water gun shooting
ceased. The girl who started the harassment
moved to North Carolina and never returned to
Franklin County High School.*

*Linda and Ruby looking for a little solace from
their daily hostile environment decided to take
that one day and visit L. M. Waid School. They
were met at the door by the L. M. Waid School
administration: the acting principal at the time
told them they were not welcomed. She said you
wanted to go to school with the whites; so you
need to stay with the whites. The white community was angry because my family thought they
were "good enough" to go to school with them.
And there were those in the black community*

angry with my family as well for choosing to attend the "white schools."

Another time when the issues on the bus had gotten to an all-time high, Dad boarded the bus and told the bus driver—who was shaking and trembling—that he was holding him personally responsible for the safety of his children. He informed the bus driver that he expected his children to board the bus and ride to school without incident.

He then followed the bus to school with a shot gun in the back window of his truck.

The superintendent of schools explained to Dad that the white children needed some time to get use to his children attending school with them. Dad explained to the superintendent they were going to get use to them fighting, because he taught his children to fight back.

There was news of a cross burning in one of the family's yards that was sending their children to the historically white schools. Cross burning was a way to intimidate and terrorize Blacks.

<u>Why the Klan Burn Crosses</u>

The practice dates back to Medieval Europe, an era the Klan idealizes as morally pure and racially homogenous. In the days before floodlights, Scottish clans set hillside crosses ablaze as symbols of defiance against military rivals or to rally troops when a battle was imminent. Though the original Klan, founded in 1866, patterned many of its rituals after those of Scottish fraternal orders, cross-burning was not part of its initial repertoire of terror.

Nevertheless, Thomas Dixon included a pivotal cross-burning scene in his 1905 novel The Clansman; he was attempting to legitimize the Klan's supposed connections to the Scottish clans. A decade later, D.W. Griffith brought The Clansman to the silver screen, eventually renaming it The Birth of a Nation.

Exhilarated by Griffith's sympathetic portrayal, Klansmen started burning crosses soon after to intimidate minorities, Catholics, and anyone else suspected of betraying the order's ideals. The first reported burning took place in Georgia on Thanksgiving Eve, 1915. They have been associated with racist violence ever since.

After hearing of the cross-burning incident, Dad visited the family and then went to the local store in Union Hall where the men gathered to chat. He said loud enough for everyone to hear, "If I see any sheets moving in my yard that are not on Helen's clothesline, they will end up with bullets in them."

In June of 1966, my parents signed a contract with Mr. A. J. Reeves, a black contractor in the county, to build a new home a stone's throw away from our current home on the same three acres of land. The contract to build the new home was for $12,200. Half was to be paid once the house was under roof and the remaining sum to be paid at completion. They took out a loan with *Bankers Trust and Company of Rocky Mount* in December 1966 for $15,000.00 at a 6% interest with a payment of $166.54 to pay over 10 years.

Move day was so exciting. Since the new brick home was merely yards away from the white home that had served our family well for 28 years, we were able to move ourselves. It was a glorious warm and sunny day. Everybody was excited and participated in the move.

The new house was one story house with a full basement. This house had a bathroom upstairs on the main floor and a bathroom in the basement. The décor in the upstairs bathroom upstairs was tastefully done in pink and the basement bathroom was decorated in aqua. At this time, our family consisted of Linda Carol, Ruby Nadean, Janis Faye, Crystal Diane, Penny Adriane and Ronald Brent. They ranged in age from 2 years to 16 years. Our new brick home had three bedrooms, a kitchen with an electric stove and a beautiful living room and dining room fully furnished with the latest style furniture. Gloria

Marie gifted Mom with an electric washer and dryer.

This was the last year Dad received a Christmas gift from his employer, the huge Methodist Church at the top of Tanyard Road. Dad and Mom explained it was because the whites did not want to see them making progress.

The last all black graduating class from Lee M. Wade graduated in 1970 which ended segregation in Franklin County.

Franklin County has seven districts. Each district is represented on the Franklin County School Board. All the school board members were appointed until 1995. Up until 1973 everyone on the school board was white. In 1973 the board was expanded to an eight-member board by adding an At-Large seat to be held by a black person. The first black appointed was Posey Lemons. He served one four-year term. When he stepped down, the black community was asked to submit names for his replacement and Dad's name was submitted among others. When he heard his name was submitted and who was making the determination, he told Linda that they were going to choose him, and he was right. He served one four-year term on the board and he made those four years count!

Paid the Same

There was only one black principal in the system at the time. He also happened to be the only principal at the time with a 10-month contract versus a 12-month contract like all the rest. Therefore, he was being paid less than the rest of the principals. Dad brought this to the board's attention and persuaded the rest of the board to give the principal a 12-month contract.

You Can't Fire Her!

A black teacher's wages were being garnished because of something her husband did and the board wanted to fire her. Dad said it was not her fault and how could they fire her for something that was not her fault when they did not fire a white man that came before the board the month before for stealing. The teacher was not fired.

CHAPTER 10

Hard Work Builds Character

I REMEMBER THAT my parents worked from "can't see to can't see." Dad would rise before daylight to be on the farm to feed cows and pigs and do other farm work. My mother was up to have breakfast on the table by 6 a.m. After breakfast she would head off to her job as a cook at Franklin County High School and Dad would head off to his job at *Rocky Mount Methodist Church*. At 2 p.m. when Mom finished up at the high school, she would go to the church and help him finish up before they headed to Ferrum College where they were both employed as janitors to clean Garber Hall.

Once they finished at Ferrum, they would stop through town and clean *First Federal Bank.* That usually got them home around 11 p.m. each night. Much of our family time centered around work. When we were around, we helped clean the church and wash black boards at Garber Hall and empty the trash.

During tobacco season the whole family participated. Everyone was out of bed, fed, dressed in long sleeve shirts, pants and a scarf on our heads to protect our hair and skin from the tobacco gum. We were in the fields as the sun rose to dry the wet leaves from the dew.

The adults and older children primed (took the yellow leaves off the bottom of the stalk which usually consisted of two to three) and the younger children carried the tobacco (took the leaves from the adults as quickly as possible not to slow them down) to the person packing the tobacco on the truck. The packer took the leaves from each carrier and packed the tobacco neatly on the truck.

As the sun dried the tobacco leaves, it fiercely dried any dampness our clothes may have received from the tobacco. Noon was lunch time. Mom, who did not work in the fields, had prepared a lunch that to this day I don't know how we ate that amount of food and went back out to work in the smoldering hot fields.

Once the priming was complete and the tobacco had been unpacked at the barn each time, the packed truck was filled, the next phase started. The tobacco at the barn was rows and rows of neatly packed leaves. There were two to three tobacco horses (which were benches where two people sat with tobacco placed between them) the two people would gather two to three leaves and hand it to the person standing in front of them that tied the tobacco with tobacco twine to a tobacco stick held up by the front of the horse. Of course, there was competition in the fields on who could prime the fastest and who carried the leaves the fastest.

However, the real competition came at the barn as who tied the fastest. As the leaves were tied, they were again neatly packed on a truck which was then taken to the tobacco barn. The tobacco was handed to two men up in the barn with their legs straddled on large post going from end to end in the barn where they hung the tobacco. From there fires were built in small fireplaces on the outside of the barn to cure the tobacco. The curing process normally took about a week.

Once all the tobacco was in the barn it was time for a celebration. . . pop (remember, Mom was from West Virginia) and peanuts or roasting hotdogs over the small fireplaces in the barn.

After the tobacco was cured, it was then taken down out of the barn and packed neatly into a large tobacco sack and taken to market. By this time, it was time to start the priming process all over again. It took about a week for two to three leaves on the bottom of the tobacco stalk to turn yellow and be ready for priming. The big prime usually took place on the weekends when all the adults were off their steady weekly paycheck jobs.

The work during the week for tobacco was chopping (removing the weeds) and topping and suckling (removing flowers that grew in the top of the tobacco and small stubs that grew between each leaf). All of this was done to ensure the growth went into the tobacco leaf itself and not in weeds, toppings and/or suckles.

The biggest lessons farming teaches and instills are the first three habits of Stephen Covey's *The 7 Habits of Highly Effective People*: "Be proactive," "Begin with the end in mind," and "Put first things first." You must plant when it is time to plant and you must harvest when it is time to harvest. There was a lot of work that the tobacco required prior to the priming season.

CHAPTER 11

Leave a Legacy

AS A LITTLE girl, on more than one occasion, I have witnessed my mother shopping in a store with clothes on the counter walk out of the store with no purchase, because one of us asked to use the bathroom and was told there was no bathroom. Mom protested too!

Prior to Dad retiring, he worked several jobs while farming. He retired in 1976 from Rocky Mount United Methodist Church (a predominately all white church), Ferrum College and First Federal Bank. We took full advantage of all these amenities that our parent's workplaces had to offer. In fact, four of my sisters: Linda, Ruby,

Faye, and Diane attended and graduated from Ferrum Junior College. They received free room and board since my parents were employees. We all attended and loved the basketball games. The players and other black students that attended Ferrum visited our home often for Sunday dinners. In the summer, my parents many grandchildren, my brother Ronnie, and I went swimming daily in Ferrum's indoor pool. Many of us learned to swim at Ferrum.

Because of Dad's character, he was well-respected by many of the white people in Rocky Mount as evidenced by the following story:

If Anyone Leaves, it Won't Be Charles!

Rocky Mount Methodist Church is approximately 2,500 sq. ft. Dad said when he first took the job as janitor, the church was filthy. He cleaned and got it spotless. You could not find a speck of dust or dirt anywhere.

After Dad had gotten the church to a point where he didn't have to do as much, he would go there Monday through Friday morning, after doing his farm work, do his cleaning, leave around 2 p.m. to go to his next job. Once when a new minister came, he told Dad they were paying him for eight hours a day and he needed to be there eight hours a day. Dad shared with him that they were paying him to keep the facility clean.

Since Dad and the minister could not agree on his hours, they did agree that the minister needed to take it before the Board. When the minister took the issue before the Board, the Board told the minister that Dad was doing an awesome job and to leave him alone. They also told him that Dad had been there for a long time and if anyone was leaving, it would not be Charles!

As he continued to share his stories of protest with us, his responsibilities grew. He provided homes for his adult children and grandchildren on and off throughout their lives. His home became home to all his grandchildren during the summer and many times throughout the year. In addition, he provided separate homes (that he owned) for his adult children and grandchildren (rent free), as well as a home for his mother during her last years, because her home had burned to the ground years before.

My parents had acquired approximately 100 plus acres of land over the years. Dad was the last to pass away. Over the years and before he passed, he made certain all his land that he had not sold belonged to his children. He wanted to make certain all his land was dispersed to his children prior to his death to ensure it was not lost or stolen due to crooks or arguments.

When we would visit home as adults, many times we would take walks with Dad on the land. He would point out each corner of the land and how it was marked. Sometimes the marks were a pile of rocks. Sometimes the marks were three marks on a tree.

He felt this was very important because many times land was stolen from blacks in the south once it was purchased with their hard work, blood, sweat and tears. So he always wanted us to know where every inch of his property started and ended. He wanted to ensure it was passed to the next generation and not stolen or lost.

CHAPTER 12

We've Come A Long Way

"I WOULD JUST like to shake his hand! I would just like to shake his hand!" had been Dad's mantra every day during the 2008 Presidential Campaign.

My then 95-year-old father had lived through overt racism where Jim Crow was the law of the land and sharecropping was the primary way for black men to make a living. Yet, there he was sitting in my living room witnessing even more history—a black man announcing his bid for the highest office in our nation.

Senator Obama's decision to run for president gave African Americans, particularly older men, a new and greater chapter in their lives. It helped, if only for a moment, soften the blows of segregation, making the "White Only" signs a little more palatable to talk about to their children and grandchildren. Like my dad they stood a little taller in humility and gratitude to witness, first-hand, the fruits of their marches, sit-ins, hose-downs, lock-ups, and refusal to give up on the truth of Dr. Martin Luther King, Jr.'s words: *I am somebody*, a creed Dad lived throughout his life and taught his children.

I retired and moved home in July 2007 and Dad moved in with me. Every night he would sit in his favorite chair, and I would sit on the couch, sipping a glass of iced tea and we would watch CNN. We were thirsty for anything and everything that had to do with this historic event. Dad was impressed with Senator Obama and believed we needed to do all we could to make sure he was elected the 44th president of the United States. I joined Senator Obama's campaign, canvassing neighborhoods, making calls, and getting people out to vote.

Senator Obama had secured the democratic nomination, and was coming to Bristol, Virginia on June 5, 2008 to announce his official bid for office. I was asked by the Grass Roots Coordinator from Roanoke to be the Grass Roots Coordinator in Franklin County and Martinsville/Henry County, affording me six VIP tickets to Senator Obama's Town Hall meeting. I knew I had to use one of those tickets to take Dad to the meeting. I had to give him this opportunity to shake Senator Obama's hand. Ruby, Faye, Diane, Ronnie, Dad and I packed the car (complete with ham biscuits and fried chicken) and set out for the three-hour trip to Bristol.

The line to get into the gym stretched around the corner as blacks, whites, children, and the elderly stood in stifling heat waiting to get inside. Ruby took Daddy to the front of the line and they allowed them to go in and be seated and save seats for the rest of us around them. Four of the five of us wore identical black tee-shirts Ruby and I had purchased at a Women's Conference in Raleigh, North Carolina a couple of months earlier. There we were, sweating, fanning, and standing tall with the pictures of Martin Luther King Jr. and Senator Obama on the front with the message: "The Dreamer and The Dream."

Our excitement was palatable as we filed into the gym. Once Senator Obama entered the gym and we all got back to our seats, a few of us touted that we had either touched him or shook his hand. Well, it was on from there! Ruby was determined that there was no way she was riding back in the car with the rest of us if she had not had the opportunity to shake his hand. We also knew there was no way for us to get Dad through a large crowd close enough to shake Senator Obama's hand without a plan.

Diane came up with the idea that Dad could give Senator Obama a gift—the hand-made wooden cane that he had made. We carved Dad's name and phone number on the cane. Next, we had to figure out a way for Dad to gift Senator

Obama the cane. We knew the format of the town halls and how they worked because we watched them on TV religiously. We knew that after his speech, Senator Obama was going to take questions from the audience.

We decided that all of us would raise our hands and when he called on one of us, we would not ask a question but let him know that our Dad had a gift for him. In the meantime, we needed Senator Obama to tell us that he loved us! So, I told everybody the best time for us to say "We love you" to Senator Obama would be as soon as everybody stopped clapping and before he had a chance to say his first word. We stood and did just that, and just as we had hoped, he said, "I love you back." We were all thrilled, excited, and thought we would faint!

Once Senator Obama completed his speech and got into the question/answer portion of the town hall, we were all waiving our hands for a question. He called on us. To this day, we debate who he specifically called on, but of course I am certain he was looking directly at me, so I took the opportunity to respond. When I was handed the mic, I said, "I have my 95-year-old Dad here with me today . . . " and before I could finish my sentence everyone in the gym rose and gave Dad a standing ovation. We were a little startled, because we were not expecting the reaction of the crowd. Once I regained my composure, I completed my sentence and told the Senator that Dad had a gift for him, and he graciously agreed to accept it. Diane started walking out of the row with Dad to help him to get to Senator Obama. Ronnie knocked her out of the way and took over. By the time Dad got to the Senator, Ruby had knocked Ronnie out of the way and taken over.

The Front Page of the Roanoke Times

Senator Obama asked Dad, how he got to be 95 and still looked as good as he did and get around so well. Dad's answer: "Hard work and three meals a day," a code that he lived by.

Dad and Senator Obama. Used by permission. © Photo Propery of
Roanoke Times. Jared Soares, Photographer

Once Dad gifted Senator Obama the cane, he
said to Dad, "It's beautiful, and, if members of
Congress don't pass my health care bill, I'm
ready. I'll whup 'em. He continued to joke, "They
better not mess with me. I'll have that stick." The
audience, full of Obama supporters, erupted in
laughter and cheers.

Now, we were all happy and satisfied and returned to our seats. Our mission had been
accomplished.

However, when the question and answer session ended, reporters from newspapers and TV stations descended upon us with tons of questions and interviews. Again, we were shocked at the reaction. A young man came out (we still don't know from where) and told Ruby that when we were finished interviewing, the Senator would like to see us. Ruby said, "What Senator?" His response, with surprise, was "Senator Obama." Ruby said, "Oh, we can stop this right now." The young man assured her that we could take our time and finish and that Senator Obama would meet with us. Then the young man approached me and shared the same information with me. As my sister, I said, "What Senator?" when he told me that once we finished our interviews, the Senator would like to see us. Again, he said in a surprised tone, "Senator Obama." I said, "Oh, we can leave right now." He assured me that we could take our time and still have time to see the Senator.

Once we were able to get away from the reporters, we were taken backstage to see Senator

Obama. When Senator Obama came out, he was ready to extend his hand and I asked him if we could have a hug. He looked a little funny, but then realized he was in the South and my sisters and I all got individual hugs. Of course, Dad and Ronnie were satisfied with a handshake. Well now it was time for a picture.

Everybody was trying to get next to the Senator, I stooped down up front and let the rest of them fight for position. I was just happy to be in the picture. Senator Obama put his hand on my shoulder. Ruby was not satisfied with that and put her hand under his hand on my shoulder.

As you can see a few of us had ink pins hanging on our shirts. When we left home, the plan was if we got close enough, we would get Senator Obama's autograph. However, once we were in his presence, no one ever thought of autographs. We never imagined we would be lucky enough to meet Senator Obama and to get pictures.

After this event, you couldn't tell Daddy anything. He was the King of the Hill. Not only did he think that, but the entire community thought it as well. He received phone calls from people as far away as Canada who saw the event on the news that evening. We love to tell the story and others love to hear it. And of course, with the storyteller my Dad was, we embellished it among ourselves.

I am nowhere to be seen in the Roanoke Times. Dad always liked to ask where I was, and I always said the others knocked me to the floor and trampled me. Dad would have a hardy laugh.

I will end this chapter by sharing the last story I have about my dad.

Who Are *You* Voting For?

My sister Ruby and I were with Dad in his bedroom as we had been many times. This time he was in a lot of pain. He kept squinching and saying his foot was in a lot of pain.

We had started having a nurse come to see him once a week. As she was doing her routine check, we explained to her his foot was in a lot of pain and we needed her to place an order for some pain medicine. Dad was not one to complain of pain.

She continued to do some other items and we let her know the priority was his pain and then she could continue with the rest of her duties.

Her response was she would need to place an order and then it would need to be picked up. I told her that was not a problem, to place the order and we would go pick it up.

We determined the pain was enough that prior to her calling in the medication, we called the ambulance. That day, Dad left home for what would be the last time.

Of course, during any good doctor or nurse visit, they must ensure the patient is lucid. So, she asked him the normal questions to determine his lucidity.

"What is your social security number?" He rattled off his social security number.

"Who is the President of the United States?" He responded with such enthusiasm that it was President Barack Obama, she decided to follow-up with another question.

"Who are you voting for?" Again, enthusiastically he said, "President Barack Obama, of course!"

So, I guess he decided he needed to determine if she was lucid and he asked her who she was voting for?

CHAPTER 13

A Time to Protest

ALL OF OUR stars point North when it comes to African American justice to secure our equal rights. We protest anytime, anywhere.

As many of my siblings, I did not realize how certain events that occurred in our childhood would impact my adult life. As number nine of ten children, I grew up understanding that protest and justice is a right, not a privilege. It is not a choice, but my God given duty and responsibility. It is *our* God given right, responsibility and duty.

The Obama campaign taught us to tell our story and showed me that my protesting has not been a choice for me. I was sent into an environment as a child that allowed me to see and experience injustice after injustice, while I was being fed confidence and protest for breakfast, lunch and dinner.

The oppressor does not get to dictate how the oppressed protest. Power is taken, it is not given. Charles always believed that one man standing could make a difference. Our household lived by one of Dr. Martin Luther King's quotes "A man can't ride your back unless it is bent." Yet Martin Luther King was not Dad's favorite hero. His favorite heroes were Adam Clayton Powell Jr, Malcolm X and Muhammad Ali. He admired men who fought back. He was not one who could participate in non-violent protest.

Because of my parents and siblings' participation and enduring support of the Virginia Democratic Party and the NAACP, including my sister Linda holding positions in those organizations, Dad was invited to Governor Doug

Wilders' inaugural ball and attended the ball with three of his daughters: Linda, Crystal, and me. His life of protest made a difference in the lives of his children, in his community, and in the great state of Virginia.

About the Author

Penny Blue is Founder and CEO of *Penny Wise Gateway, LLC*, a leadership training and consulting company specializing in Leadership Strategy Development, Management and Leadership Development and Project Management. Before becoming a trainer, Penny worked as a Delivery Project Executive at IBM where she engaged in data center operations, customer care, application development/maintenance, distribution systems, databases, process improvement, human resources, and financial management.

Following in the footsteps of her father, Ms. Blue utilized her excellent interpersonal skills and passion during the 2008 presidential campaign as a grass roots coordinator for Franklin, Henry and Pittsylvania counties. She helped turn Virginia "Blue" and provide the biggest congressional upset in the nation sending a Democrat to Congress in the 5th District by unseating a 6-term congressman. She galvanized communities, to recruit, register, and turnout some of the most unlikely voters in large numbers. She then parlayed that experience to the 2010 Census First Count Committee where she achieved excellent first count success.

Ms. Blue is one of the founding members of the Friends of Booker T. Washington National Monument and served as President over the past eight years. She also holds a position on the Franklin County School Board once held by her dad.

She resides in Virginia.

References

Chapter 1: Repeating History

- The Willie Lynch Letter. Retrieved from: http://www.finalcall.com/artman/publish/Perspec-tives_1/Willie_Lynch_letter_The_Making_of_a_Slave.shtml
- Bacon's Rebellion. Retrieved from: https://en.wikipedia.org/wiki/Bacon%27s_Rebellion
- Research Findings on the Traumatic Stress Effects of Terrorism https://www.ptsd.va.gov/professional/treat/type/terrorism_research.asp
- The Roots of the Ku Klux Klan. Retrieved from: https://en.wikipedia.org/wiki/Ku_Klux_Klan
- Reconstruction and Its Aftermath. Retrieved from: https://memory.loc.gov/ammem/aaohtml/exhibit/aopart5.html

- The History of Jim Crow. Retrieved from: https://en.wikipedia.org/wiki/Portal:Civil_rights_movement/Selected_article/2
- Slavery in the U.S. Prison System. Retrieved from: https://www.aljazeera.com/indepth/opinion/2017/09/slavery-prison-system-170901082522072.html
- Trump Wishes He Could Destroy Obama's Legacy. He Hasn't. And Won't. Jonathan Chait. May 20, 2015. NewYorkMag. Retrieved from: http://nymag.com/intelligencer/2018/05/trump-wishes-he-could-destroy-obamas-legacy-he-hasnt.html
- The Discriminatory Wage Gap. Retrieved from: https://www.epi.org/press/black-white-wage-gaps-larger-today-than-in-1979-due-primarily-to-discrimination/

Chapter 2: Roots: The Family Tree

- Family Tree Census. *The Ancient Arms of Mattox,* Mattox-Skipper, Cassandra
- Master-Slave Relations. Retrieved from: https://www.finalcall.com/artman/publish/editorials/article_103714.shtml

- Purchase Deed, 100 Acres, Franklin County Court House, Book 52, page 350, dated January 12, 1903
- Purchase Deed, 3 Acres, Franklin County Court House, Book 128, page 19, dated March 1954
- Forty Acres and a Mule. Retrieved from: https://www.americanhistoryusa.com/topic/forty-acres-and-a-mule/

Chapter 3: Freedom is Not Free

- The Horace Greely Letter. Retrieved from: http://www.abrahamlincolnonline.org/lincoln/speeches/greeley.htm
- U.S. 1860 Census. Retrieved from: https://www.census.gov/library/publications/1864/dec/1860a.html
- Lincoln's August 26, 1863 Conkling Letter. Retrieved from: http://www.abrahamlincolnonline.org/lincoln/speeches/conkling.htm
- Congress Confiscates Confederates' Slaves. Sean Wilentz. July 16, 2012 NYTimes.com The Opinion Pages. Retrieved from: https://opinionator.blogs.nytimes.com/201

2/07/16/congress-confiscates-confederates-slaves/

- THE EMANCIPATION PROCLAMA-TION 166 ... pp. 43-44; Lerone Bennett, Ebony Pictorial History of Black America, Vol I, (Nashville,. 1971), p. 71.

Chapter 4: Short-Lived Changes

- The Appearance of Change. Retrieved from: https://www.yourvoteyourvoicemn.org/past/communities/african-americans-past/reconstruction-era-1865-1877
- White Supremacy. Segregation Had to Be Invented. Retrieved from: https://www.theatlantic.com/business/archive/2017/02/segregation-invented/517158/
- Jim Crow Laws by State. Retrieved fro: https://en.wikipedia.org/wiki/List_of_Jim_Crow_law_examples_by_state
- Interracial Marriage in Virginia. Retrieved from: https://en.wikipedia.org/wiki/Loving_v._Virginia
- The Plan. Retrieved from: https://advancementproject.org/news/civil

-rights-groups-file-amicus-brief-in-
virginia-restoration-of-voting-rights-case/

Chapter 5: Racism from the Top

- William Trotter's Meetings with Woodrow Wilson. Retrieved from:
  https://www.theatlantic.com/politics/archi
  ve/2015/11/wilson-legacy-racism/417549/
- The Birth of a Nation. Retrieved from:
  https://en.wikipedia.org/wiki/The_Birth_o
  f_a_Nation
- Eugene Williams' Drowning. Retrieved
  from:
  https://www.history.com/topics/black-
  history/chicago-race-riot-of-1919
- White Primaries. Retrieved from:
  https://en.wikipedia.org/wiki/White_prim
  aries

Chapter 6: Separate and Unequal

- Not Entitled to Freedom. Retrieved from:
  https://collectiveliberation.org/wp-
  con-
  tent/uploads/2013/01/Smith_Patriarchy_a
  nd_Privilege.pdf
- How the Klan Got Its Hood. Retrieved
  from:

https://newrepublic.com/article/127242/kl
an-got-hood

Chapter 7: Went In Coming Out

- Purchase Deed, Franklin County Courthouse, Book 101, Page 290, July 24, 1944
- The Master Race. Retrieved from:
  https://en.wikipedia.org/wiki/Master_race

Chapter 8: Life in Virginia

- Purchase Deed, Franklin County Courthouse, Book 128, Page 19, March 5, 1954

Chapter 9: Education: Freedom of Choice

- The Right to Fairness: Retrieved from:
  https://www.nps.gov/nr/twhp/wwwlps/les
  sons/121brown/121facts2.htm
- Prince Edwards County Population. Retrieved from:
  https://www.americanprogress.org/issues/
  education-k-
  12/reports/2017/07/12/435629/racist-
  origins-private-school-vouchers/
- Rosenwald Schools. Retrieved from:
  https://preservationvirginia.org/our-
  work/architectural-rosenwald-school-
  survey/

- Freedom of Choice. Retrieved from: https://www.virginiahistory.org/collections-and-resources/virginia-history-explorer/civil-rights-movement-virginia/green-decision
- Why the Klan Burn Crosses. Retrieved from: https://slate.com/news-and-politics/2002/12/why-does-the-ku-klux-klan-burn-crosses.html

Made in the USA
Columbia, SC
18 January 2021

31159191R00114